To Mrs. Olsen, who told me to write through everything

Introduction

People tend to use the term *journey* when describing the last four years of my life. Though I know that this is said to imply that there was a beginning, a middle, and an end that followed the rigorous plot of any heroic cycle, it was never a *journey* to me; it was simply the last four years of my life. When I arrived home from Spaulding Rehabilitation Center in Charlestown, Massachusetts, I was frequently asked what I had learned about myself and the world around me. Well, the "wise-beyond-her-years," "mature" thirteen-year-old me had no idea. It has taken until now for me to finally grasp what it is I took from the experiences, and it came with the understanding that an end is nowhere near in sight. Perhaps I will never find my "ending," but then again, do any of us?

Hormonal, awkward, and living my best life, my teenage years so far have been a confusing jumble of changing perspectives. I can only report what I know now to be true, so I suggest you not enter this memoir of mine with the notion that you will come across some revelation; rather, I suggest you expect to hear a story. Perhaps with this story you will think, find something, learn something. But know that despite my *journey*, I know as little about life as you do.

Upbringing

My upbringing was relatively normal, at least in comparison to those around me in Falmouth, Maine. Ever since I can remember, I've had a loving family, close friends, satisfactory grades, and a pretty high level of self-confidence. Maybe the first twelve years of my life were just some prolonged "calm before the storm."

I was born in Portland, Maine, and have lived just a town over, in Falmouth, ever since. I have been extremely fortunate as families go. I was blessed at birth with two wonderful parents who have been both my mentors and my best friends, and if that wasn't enough, I also have an older brother I love infinitely. These particular people will continue to have an enormous role throughout this process, but if at any time my love for them is a question in your mind, I can assure you that my heart was and always has been with them.

People usually describe difficult life events, or more specifically the recovery from difficult life events, by remembering all of those who went through it alongside them. You see, the cliché that friends and family are what get you out of dark times definitely has some merit. I genuinely feel as though I would not have half the confidence or positivity that I have now if I hadn't had such strong relationships with all of these people in my life.

As for me, well, I'll start this portion from as early as I can recall. From the very beginning, I was extroverted. I loved the notion of entertaining others solely by expressing myself, so I never really shied away from that. One would assume that interest would lie in the performance arts, and although that is now true, it certainly was not at the time. All I wanted to do was sports. I was enthralled by the contest of it all, something I figure is hereditary, considering my mother's competitive nature. There was a time when I was playing five organized sports at a time, and that was fifth grade alone… I wasn't even trying to build a resumé.

Involved in a variety of clubs and activities, my life seemed pretty average; it was a positive average, like the average that you would assume fortunate, privileged, and extroverted kids have. Little did I know that my life would soon become extraordinary.

It was in the sixth grade that I finally decided to run on a track team. I had always known that I could outrun the other girls during tryouts and that, to put it bluntly, my only real basketball worth stemmed from the fact that I always seemed to get on the other end of the court faster than anyone else. Track gave me the very first thing that set me apart, at least from my own perspective.

The very first day of indoor track practice, I remember, we were asked to warm up. I had on a T-shirt and gym shorts even though everyone else seemed to be decked out in expensive headbands, fancy leggings, and dry fit shirts with the logo from some race they had previously competed in. I never really considered the possibility that the appearance worries of middle school would seep into track as well. Nonetheless I buddied up with a girl I had known for quite some time, though mostly just through mutual friends.

Delaney is best described as "the happiest person you'll ever meet." The most amazing thing about her is not her happiness, though. It is instead the consistent happiness—a genuinely optimistic attitude that I feel so few people possess. She had been a runner from a very young age and was immensely talented. I envied just about everything you could use to describe her. Eventually, I'd be referred to as "Delaney's friend," but before you panic for my twelve-year-old self-esteem, let me explain.

The coach of the Falmouth Middle School track team is one of the most influential human beings that I've been worthy of having in my life. I knew that while writing this, I would likely talk too much about individuals, but if you are going to understand anything about my track years, let it be Coach D.

He worked alongside other coaches throughout the years, though he had continually been staying with the team. He knew what he was talking about. Before I even laced up my shoes, my teammates had been filling me in about what he was like. All of them had very pleasant things to say about him, but I recall one of the older kids telling me he was observant. As someone who thought that I might be interesting to an observer, I liked this notion. To get to the point, I'll spoil the ending for you: I was observed.

He approached Delaney at the end of the practice to ask about me. Then, for a week he called me "Delaney's friend" until I had outrun a group of the fastest boys at our school. I guess that earned me my name.

Long story short, I fell madly in love with track. I had joined the school's theatre company and performed in the sixth-grade show, although I knew that I'd pursue track when given the choice. Maybe it was simply that headstrong mind-set about that one decision that led to my injury, who really knows. Either

7

way, I believe that the universe knew that track was not in the cards for me, even if running competitively gave me some of the most empowering memories I may ever receive. I felt confident, needed, respected, and talented. I didn't feel anything like it for a long while afterward.

Maine Medical Center

"Pericles in Athens"—that was the title of the five-paragraph essay I had due for my social studies teacher the next day. Stressed out of my mind, I arrived home after track practice with only one goal: finishing that essay. The pressure on sixth graders these days didn't cause my injury, but someone should seriously look into the amount of homework students get assigned.

Anyways, I digress. The only importance to my focus on this assignment is that perhaps I didn't feel anything because my mind was elsewhere. That's what some people speculate. A few of the medical professionals believe my injury must have been caused by something that hit my shoulder during practice that day. Yes, because the necessity to protect one's shoulders in track is so dire.

I may come off as angered by this assumption, and that's because I am. Throughout this experience one key thing I learned is that nobody can pinpoint what is going on in someone's body when it's not *their* body. I don't believe that my track practice was the reason for my injury. The public forum debater in me argues that having no other just reason makes my con statement invalid, but there were other reasons; it's just that none of those reasons seemed right either. I'll let you hypothesize yourselves, though the only fact of the matter is that it all began while I was writing an essay.

The exact time that the pain struck my right shoulder was 4:55 p.m. on May 21, 2014. I know this because it is still spelled out on the top of the document I was working on. The revision history proves that the last edit I made before anxiously approaching my living room couch was at that time. At least I could change *was* to *were* before I had to stop; it's that kind of attention to detail that never fails to exceed the standards.

Accompanying the sharp pain in my right shoulder was an instant recap of my day. I had no recollection of injuring it, so I simply asked for my dad to bring me a heating pad. I lay on the couch for about two minutes before my dad came in and suggested I go upstairs and rest for a bit. Thank whatever God you believe in that I declined. With tears building up, the pain worsened, and the options transitioned from going upstairs to going to our local urgent care facility. Then, the most surreal experience of my life happened in a matter of ninety seconds.

The pain that stretched about an inch on my shoulder rapidly spread from the right side of my body to the left. Every muscle and nerve seemed to tense up, and I couldn't release. After an agonizing thirty seconds or so of panic, I was paralyzed.

To this day I cannot describe what being completely paralyzed feels like, but I know how I described it to the kind EMTs who picked me up at my house. It's rather unfortunate that I screamed their heads off like I did.

I told them that it felt like I was floating. I saw my body but could not move or feel anything. I was entirely a set of eyes looking down upon a body that I couldn't believe was my own. It felt like I was flailing my limbs around, trying to find the ground, but I later found out that I hadn't moved at all. My sensation and ability to move had vanished in just over a minute. The EMTs tried to lift me onto a stretcher. As they picked me up above the couch, an unreal terror rose within me. I thought I was falling to the ground with every motion they made because I saw only my core suspended and couldn't see their hands. I was certain they'd drop me, but they successfully got me into the ambulance.

This is when my panic was matched with an internal dialogue that assured me nothing could possibly be wrong. I tried calming down, though I continued interrogating the EMTs, asking them countless times if what I was experiencing was normal. They seemed to be genuine human beings, but they would not answer my question. I tried to relax. I shut my eyes and then opened them as I was being pushed into the ambulance alongside my father.

It was a nice day, the sun was shining, and the bare trees rustled with the wind. This provoked a second of pleasantness. With a deep breath, I anticipated the gust of wind that passed through the trees clashing with the warmth of the sun above. I felt neither. Reality sank back in throughout the ambulance ride.

At Maine Medical Center in Portland, the "why" of what had happened was not really the priority. My goal is not to criticize Maine Med in the terms of their medical capabilities, but sure, I'll call them out on this one instance. If you ever find yourself giving in to the false conception that doctors know anything more about the world than you do, remember that I was a healthy, twelve-year-old girl who had never been sick a day in my life, and no team of doctors knew anything more than I did about what was about to happen.

Consumed by the fear that this was more than a simple effect of dehydration, I hardly could take in what was going on around me. I recall begging doctors to fill me in, but more often than not they ignored this request. Even on *Grey's Anatomy* I had never seen doctors look so confused, and I watched that show when Meredith was still an intern. I can picture it as if I'm living it now. I was lying in a hospital bed wondering what the hell was going on, yet trying to keep in tune with the craziness of it all. Then, my greatest fear was about to come true.

I should have known better. Despite my claustrophobia, an MRI was certainly not the worst medical fate I'd encounter. Nonetheless, this MRI marked the end of my innocence. Here I realized that being naive was no longer an option. They say you grow up through divorce, family troubles, and friend drama, and they say those experiences are where children lose their ability to "just be kids," as my father would say. As for me, I had maintained my imaginative and optimistic mentality even through those sorts of changes and life events, but my youthfulness still died too soon. My childhood died in that metal chamber.

They didn't know what had caused the injury or illness, which seemed to be worsening, but they knew it had started in my shoulder. With the intention of imaging what was going on in that area of my upper back, they put my paralyzed and hardly functioning body through a five-and-a-half-hour MRI that ended in the dark hours of the early morning.

Nobody can accompany you in an MRI. Before you are transferred on a stiff board of back-aching proportions, you are stripped of your family, your clothes, and your recognizable surroundings. Once the transfer is complete, you are stripped of your sanity. Tubes that were attached through IVs and other means of injections were my only company as I lay there, watching my childhood seep through my skull.

MRIs emit an eardrum-bursting noise as soon as the imaging begins. I had earplugs securing the inner sections of my ears, but I still grimaced in pain. A voice that seemed to come from the skies above spoke to me. It questioned whether I was in pain, and I delivered the most pathetic lie of my life so far… and I once told a teacher that my cat ripped up my homework in the fourth grade. I faintly released a "No," which led to the machine restarting its terrorizing screams. For first three hours, I thought about whether I'd miss the track meet on the following day.

Then the right earplug decided to slip down just far enough below the opening of my ear so that it would no longer provide any noise-canceling properties. I tried to get the attention of the man who had spoken to me earlier, but when I tried to formulate a word, I couldn't produce any sounds. When I was younger, one of my neighbors used to cover himself in leaves on Halloween so that he could hide on the ground as trick-or-treaters went by. I was once one of his victims, and I remember dropping my candy and feeling the pounding of my heart racing for the rest of the night. Even so, this portion of my first MRI was the scariest moment of my life.

Although I now know that this MRI lasted approximately five hours, I do not remember the rest. From then onward, my only other clear memory from those early hours of the morning was of my dad when the nurses rolled me out of the double doors that had separated us earlier. He was smiling, but there was a very obvious pain in his eyes.

Plenty of other MRIs and tests followed: an angiogram, a spinal tap, and an abundance of blood tests. Four years later I still have no idea what any of those are; I just know that they were unpleasant. The physical hurt they inflicted was less painful, however, than the pain that accompanied the results from each one, which never seemed to tell us anything more about what was going on than we already knew. At some point, it was determined that I had had a spinal cord stroke. There were a variety of other possibilities, but this was supposedly the most accurate diagnosis they had for what had occurred.

Despite the diagnosis, there still seemed to be an unsettling amount of confusion surrounding what steps were necessary for my recovery. My parents tell me that the doctors at

Maine Med pulled them aside and told them they wanted to put a tube down my throat, thus putting me on life support; the doctors also said they assumed I'd never come off of it. They didn't know my family and me.

We were determined to fight before we even knew we'd have to. My parents called hospitals in Boston until they somehow scored me a bed in Tufts Medical Center's Pediatric Intensive Care Unit. I'm not entirely sure how this went down, but I do remember the relief of knowing that I'd be going somewhere else. My doctors insisted that I get there by helicopter because of my deteriorating condition, but with little time and no helicopters available, I ended up on a way-less-cool ambulance.

Before I left, my softball coach, Matt Rogers, visited twice in the two days I was in Portland. He brought with him DVDs of classic movies, which I watched all the way through and used as a distraction. In my head I contemplated the underlying messages of *Dirty Dancing* and was admittedly freaked out by *The Goonies*. I thought about what I'd do if I were a kid in that movie… Then I thought about how embarrassing it'd be if my final thought was about my Goonies strategy.

If my last thought was going to be about my Goonies game plan, at least it wouldn't have been at all concerned with what the IV tubes were feeding into my blood or whether doctors thought I'd ever move again. My mind was preoccupied, thanks to Coach Rogers. I think the only reason that the possibility of permanent paralysis never depressed me very much was that it was too inconceivable for me to understand at the time. What you don't know really can't hurt you, I guess, and I really didn't know the realness of what was ahead. Thankfully, by the time I did, I was ready to take it on with everything I had.

This ambulance ride was weird, let me tell you. Out of everything that happened four years ago, it is perhaps the strangest memory I have in comparison to what actually occurred. I've been told that while in my bed in the ambulance, I lost almost all of my ability to breathe. I was in terrible shape, connected to wires and tubes that barely kept me alive for the two-hour ride. All I remember is that they brought a little TV in so that I could watch *Frozen* on the way down. Nothing makes a near-death experience better than Olaf does.

Tufts

I remember lying in bed for the first few days at Tufts. I started to miss people. So far, the trials had been seemingly individual. The MRI trapped me in a cage where I was alone with my thoughts and a body that was mine, yet unrecognizable. The IVs and feeding tubes were forced into me by a variety of doctors, many of whom I'd see for that dreadful moment and then never see again. All of the decisions about my treatments were made behind thick plastic curtains just permeable enough for me to see people running their fingers through their hair in a display of stress and helplessness. I think my display was just one of loneliness.

My parents told me that Sam, seventeen at the time, was in the building—something rather miraculous, considering the fact that my brother is not a fan of the hospital scene—and that he wanted to come talk to me. I'll never know what this moment was like for my brother. I cannot imagine what it would be like to walk into a room and see him hooked up to a million machines, hardly able to breathe on his own. I guess he lives with that memory of me every day.

I excitedly told my parents that I wanted to see him, and I have a vivid picture in my mind of the moment he came into the room. Despite my joy at seeing him, though, I almost immediately asked him to leave. I don't know why I didn't want him there anymore. Perhaps it was the shame I still carried about my physical appearance; I was awfully exposed, and felt like my body was some patchwork of a Frankenstein monster stitched together by needles and devices. It very well could have been a mental battle though, too. I could have been overwhelmed by the brokenness I was showing to one of the people I love most in this universe. I very clearly remember how my heart ached when he came in, as his sympathetic attempt to keep smiling reminded me of how he had last seen me in a track T-shirt and gym shorts.

I never look at this moment as a weakness. I try not to associate that word with any of my experiences, but this one in particular is never something I've dwelled on. This moment was a test of the waters where I sank my feet into a hot tub too quickly and burned myself. I simply made a miscalculation regarding how ready I was to face the world as I knew it. I was aware that I'd be able to see my brother whenever I wanted to, and that if next time I made it to a minute, that would in and of itself become a feat. I eventually saw the people I knew and loved for hours at a time. My visits with people became my therapy sessions.

I've really never seen a therapist since my injury. This is likely because of my arrogance and persistent desire to conceal my feelings and emotions, but I've been able to use a lack of time as a good excuse. I've been advised on countless occasions to speak to someone, but I just never have had the need. In no way do I mean to offend the practice. I know many people who find therapy to be a necessity in their lives and who go for their own reasons.

When others have suggested it to me, I've never underestimated its helpfulness or value to others; I've just never wanted it for myself.

My therapy truly was seeing my friends. One by one I'd convince them that I was still the girl who loved sports, school, and making smart-ass comments in serious situations to lighten the mood, and every person who regained comfortableness around me made me more comfortable around them. I also found healing properties in writing. I started writing journal entries on my iPod Touch when I was first regaining mobility in my left hand. I never wrote much at a time because hitting the right letters was stressful and took ages, but I made a start on it. Eventually, the writing became easier and this book was formed. So basically you're reading my diary... Feel special.

Just like any good diary, there were a lot of humiliating and uncomfortable parts of my time at Tufts. I used to be nervous talking about this sort of thing, but I've discovered that it's surprisingly freeing. My body was not in my control. My body was a sacred, damaged, and fighting entity in desperate need of professional attention in all aspects. When I had to be washed in bed by nurses or when I was taking showers with a few of them, I wasn't ever really that embarrassed. I sort of separated from my own skin. I was tired and relatively powerless, and thus accepted the bathing concepts pretty early on.

When they'd wash me in bed, I couldn't feel much. It was like watching someone else's body being washed by rags and hot water, so it didn't feel very attached to me in a way. By the time I started to feel on my left side, I had overcome the awkwardness and discomfort of the situation enough to enjoy the feeling of water again. The heat was almost unbearable, because I had a severe hypersensitivity to temperatures. The nerves were being exposed to the world again, and that was apparently too much for them to handle. Fun fact: I still have a pretty significant amount of this sort of sensitivity on my right side, even though I have paralysis only in my leg and right hand. If you see me wearing a million layers in the winter months, just know that half of my body feels ridiculous and the other half needs to not feel like it's freezing.

The initial awkwardness of exploring my nerve function through bathing was not particularly fun, I must admit. I was twelve and afraid of my changing body anyways, and now all of a sudden it was changing way more than it ever had. Fifth-grade health class had prepared me for a lot, but it had not prepared me for this.

The worst night of my life happened when my "resilient attitude" had yet to fully develop. I had been at Tufts for only two or three days when I recognized the concerning state into which I had fallen. I try to balance the positivity and the negativity throughout this book while describing what happened, but if I try to stay as truthful as I intend to, the truth must be written as it occured. I struggled writing this section more than any other, and I still don't think I've gotten it quite right. I want to give out two notes before I get into it.

This is my experience and nobody else's. Everyone handles the challenges in their lives differently, and my purpose for telling you how I handled mine in this situation is solely to reveal an honest recollection of my injury. I felt that if I were to exclude this detail, I would be doing a grave disservice to anyone else who may hit these lows in their lifetimes.

I am not asking for sympathy, and I have reached a point in my life where the thoughts that I had here no longer burden me like they did this one late evening. I am doing well mentally now, and chose to write the next portion as a letter to my parents to best relay how personal this is to me.

Dear Mom and Dad,

Here is the inner monologue I'm sure you'd hope I would never have. To exclude this portion from my story would be unjust, and although I've considered it many times, here it is. I figured that if someone read this and was going through anything like what we went through, they deserve to hear the raw truth. My truth is confusing, complex, and certainly not completely described in this text. The truth for both of you is equally varied and individual, so I present this portion to the world knowing now its value and importance to my personal experience.

I was in an incredible amount of pain. The pain was an evil combination of physical and mental distress at this point, and I felt as though I didn't even have dignity to hold on to anymore. Who I was existed only in the past. Unaware of what a future without my old self would contain, my mind resorted to the worst. Sure, I had struggles with self-image before my injury—most of the girls my age were dealing with some level of it; this was different. This was a pure and unmistakable hatred for my body. For whatever reason, my physical being had decided to start a battle against itself, and I was no match. Everything I had ever loved I thought was taken from me, and I was too young to recognize the beauty that still existed. I was convinced that my fate was total paralysis for the rest of my life, and I was petrified.

I thought that track was who I was. I thought that performing and dancing and singing was who I was. I thought that even if those things weren't who I was, I was something that moved and talked. I thought that moving and talking was necessary for loving and feeling. I couldn't understand the importance of life in this state. I thought that life was much more than anything I'd be able to get back.

I had no walls to build up anymore. I want to say I was naturally strong enough to win this fight, but I wasn't. This fight was something that I didn't think I could see through. This fight was made to break me.

My hospital bed was a river of dead nerves and pain. Tubes and wires poured medicine into my veins that drowned me faster. You both had thrown life jackets of love and support into my bed, yet I still struggled to stay afloat. You both gifted me with constant care and attention, and thanking you for this is something I will never be able to do in full. I don't think that a parent's sacrifice can ever be thanked properly. There was nothing more you could've done to bring me out of this sadness. I was dragged by pain into a void that enveloped me and held tight.

I wanted to stop trying. I wanted to stop trying so badly. There were IVs attached to parts of my arm that I thought I could pull. I thought maybe, in my hardly staying alive state, a pull could make everything easier.

I stared and tried, but I couldn't yet move my arm enough. So, I thought to myself that I'd try it again tomorrow. By the time tomorrow came, I had lost interest. Something magnificent was watching me that night. Something was familiar with that void. Something gave me Nurse Suzi the next day, and Nurse Suzi reminded me of what I had to live for. She shined light on you two, on my friends, and on the community that was aching for my pain. I saw love in a new way. I saw love as something you two had given me in a way that no human could ever dream to. My gratitude is never ending.

I love you,

Haley

Nurse Suzi O'Hara deserves a book written solely about her. This outspoken, Iggy Azalea–jamming, doesn't-give-a-shit Bostonian may very well have saved my life. On the very first day I met her, she came into my room like any other nurse. I remember that she was number five—she was the fifth woman to come into my room and reveal my bony, pale, and naked body to wash me.

I never thought that my life of caring for my personal hygiene by myself would ever just suddenly change. These women, whom I'd never met, were scrubbing my skin and assisting me when I had no control over my bodily functions. I know I had no reason to, but I've never been so ashamed. Every day that my body was laid out in front of my view, I watched someone else's hand clean my fatless stomach. Over the course of my stay at Tufts alone I had lost sixteen pounds. I'm not saying that a stroke is an ideal weight loss regimen, but I can guarantee you that it works faster than Weight Watchers. I hated every square inch. Every time my stomach would sink just a little more into the well of ribs, a piece of me seemed to disintegrate into nothingness. It felt as though I spent every few hours staring at someone else's body being violated by strangers. Then, I met this number five.

She waltzed into my room and sent my parents away. I knew that the dreadful reveal of my body was fast approaching. She followed the procedure that all of them did. She brought in her table on wheels with various loofahs and toothbrushes still in their wrappers. I then awaited the question that they would all ask— "So, how are you?" to which I'd always sarcastically respond, "*Great*," because I was bitchy and to an extent, rightfully so. Instead of the typical greeting, however, Nurse Suzi confidently asked, "How're ya?" Before I could answer, she went a bit off script and noted that I "must be feeling pretty shitty because you're here." She wasn't wrong.

She then asked if she could play her new Iggy album, and despite my sufficient knowledge of modern pop music at the time, I didn't know who she was referring to. I figured,

Why not? without really knowing what to expect. Then, she blasted a rap album.

Yes, you have read this in the correct order. Setting: A twelve-year-old girl depressed out of her mind in a bed of excruciating pain and shame / Subject: A loud, in-your-face optimist with a desire to play music in a PICU with patients and families next door / Me: Saying "whatever" because I figured this could only go poorly, and I thrive on awkward situations.

In the midst of this wild introduction, she asked me whether I knew the origin of the name *Iggy Azalea*. I did not. She taught me that it was formed like a stripper name: Iggy was her first pet, and Azalea was the street name of her first home. I responded with "Stripes Summit." Suzi was noticeably confused, and I told her that'd be my name using her formula. At once, we both laughed hysterically.

I don't know whether it was the silliness of the idea that any stripper would want to go by the least sexy name possible—Stripes

Summit—or that my first response to her less-than-appropriate story was to participate, but we could not stop laughing. I remember that laughing was painful. My feeding tube seemed to bounce every time I'd move my throat around, which is not a fun feeling, but I was not at all worried about it. I was laughing like I'd known laugher: the kind with a friend or with my dad watching *SNL*, and that was a wonderful thing. I had gone from the undoubtedly darkest moment of my life to one of the brightest in less than twenty-four hours.

I'm going to ask you to pause in your reading for a moment. If you know a pediatric nurse, I beg of you to thank them immediately. There may be no more noble a profession than nursing. Nurse Suzi was my absolute rock during everything, but every nurse I encountered had similar qualities, and each brought love and compassion into their work. It took me awhile to figure out how I'd best articulate my appreciation for nurses and what they do. To me, these nurses are your parents when your real parents are trying to juggle the sudden and unpredictable experience of having a sick child. They step in with grace and experience to help families cope with this new version of life, doing whatever it takes to give comfort and assistance. Nurses are the walking, breathing angels that live among us, and we should all be really thankful for them.

Suzi encouraged me to take on the world. Whenever I thought I could handle something, she'd suggest I do the next thing. The initial phases of my physical recovery were focused on fixing my breathing, my ability to eat and drink, and my ability to talk, all while maintaining stable vital signs (blood pressure, temperature, and so on). She convinced me that I could do it all.

One day, she rolled a giant leather chair on wheels into my room. By this point, Suzi was familiar with my attitudes and honesty. I remember glancing at it for seconds before blurting out, "Nope." You can probably guess that my rejection didn't halt Suzi's plan to get me on it.

A team of nurses brought in an intimidatingly large lifting contraption. Unenthused, I complied after a few minutes of seemingly rehearsed persuasion. The device was like a massive sling. My father and a few nurses worked together to fit me on it. However, there was no neck or head support.

The sling portion stretched from the backs of my knees to my shoulders, leaving my calves and head hanging off. My dad held my head, and we were ready to move. I trust my dad with my life, but I was so afraid his hand would slip. I knew that if my head were to fall backward, my neck wouldn't be able to hold it up and it would snap. I knew this because my dad used to say whenever we were in the refrigerator aisle of Hannaford, "Did you know the human head weighs eight pounds? That's almost as much as a gallon of milk."

Some of my memories from my days at Tufts have nearly faded, but this one is as clear as day. I told my dad not to drop me about a thousand times in the thirty seconds it took to get from bed to chair. Despite my distress, I made it. I remember my relief and Suzi's smug grin.

The chair soon became my mode of transportation. I was able to escape my room in the chair on three occasions. The first was with Suzi just a day after we figured out how to get me transferred from the bed to the chair. She rolled me through the hallways until we got to the ground floor. This was definitely not allowed, but it totally should've been.

She rolled that huge chair into the Au Bon Pain at the medical center and had my dad buy me a chocolate croissant. I couldn't eat it at the time and complained that it'd be stale when I'd be able to. Suzi assured me that it wouldn't be, which was absolutely her way of hinting at the next trial we were going to take on: eating sans feeding tube up my nose.

Before I could start eating anything by myself without tubes involved (a luxury, really), I had to prove to the doctors that I was capable of it. I had to successfully execute a "chew and swallow" test with graham crackers and apple juice. Understanding that this test meant I could be reunited with my lost love, real food, I was prepared to demolish a graham cracker. Luckily, it went down without much trouble. The juice followed easily after.

Suzi seemed serious about putting me back on the feeding tube overnight once more despite my success, and sure, that was probably the best idea, but I was not for it. I could eat by myself now. I still couldn't really taste anything because whatever medicine was being pumped into me still made everything taste distinctly like metal, but I could feel textures in my mouth and at least pretend.

There's a type of occupational therapy called "mirror therapy" that is used to try to trick the brain into thinking your body is moving by placing a mirror between your right and left hands. So, when I would move my left hand, it would appear in the mirror as though both of my hands were moving, when in reality, my right hand remained still behind the mirror. Similarly, when my nurse said she would allow me to get off the feeding tube only if I could eat

3000 calories by the evening, my dad raced over to the Chinatown McDonald's down the street. I was READY to trick my brain into tasting an ungodly amount of McNuggets.

Turns out that just as with mirror therapy, results don't show right away. So, it was a challenge. Let me tell you right now, that was not the best meal I've ever had. Even so, I ate all of it. Shamelessly. When I was growing up, the Italian side of my family was shocked when I'd finish heaps of my grandmother's spaghetti despite my age and size, so I was trying to channel that version of myself ("version" as if that isn't me all of the time).

I think Suzi doubted my abilities, because she seemed a bit defeated when I called her into my room to tell her I was finished. Miraculously, I was allowed to sleep without the feeding tube and to see how I was doing the next morning. When morning came, I was not only doing just as well as I had been the night before, but excited for a big, metal-tasting breakfast.

Catherine was one of my only friends to visit
Tufts. Medicine is powerful, sure, but the joy
she brought me was all-encompassing. She and
I hadn't been friends for very long, but we were
extremely close. We had spent most of our time
together making jokes in class, watching *Family
Guy*, and marveling at our countless similarities.
The prospect of seeing her for the first time was
frightening because I couldn't help but think
that all of that would be lost. She was a friend
who was given to me at this time by some
powerful force above who knew I needed a
strong young woman my age by my side. She
was a gift, and I can't begin to visualize my
recovery without her energy and positivity. I got
into the chair for the second time because I
didn't want my best friend to see me in a bed
fighting for my life. No, she would see me
fighting sprawled out in a comfortable leather
chair.

Catherine exhibited the exact opposite
behavior I had expected, in the best way
possible. She didn't look scared, surprised, or

upset to see me attached to a million tubes and loud machines. She simply looked happy to see me.

Throughout our visit, we read through cards, rolled around in the chair for a while, and ate fun snacks that started to remind me of non-metal-like tastes. Catherine brought our favorite snack with her, tasteless yet addictive Nut-Thins. With my arm and hand movement on my left side at the time, I was functioning just enough to reach into the bag to grab one. I still couldn't move anything on the right half of my body, but I thought I'd show off. Boy, was that a mistake.

The second my father saw that I could grab a cracker on my own, he and Catherine would not help feed them to me anymore. I know, right? Terrible people. So that became a fun little game that I hated but accepted as a consequence of my actions. They thought it was amusing, and I remember Catherine specifically mentioning that it'd be a funny story one day. It's been four years... Still not laughing, guys.

What they did next is pretty entertaining though.

My dad made a sticker that said "Haley" with a little arrow next to it and put it on my chair so that it pointed to me. I couldn't move enough to remove it, and this made them crack up. Good thing I eventually gained as much mobility as I did, because that would have been a really sick story if I had never been able to reach it. Imagine that: getting to a sticker would've become my entire life's goal and my best friend and father would've been to blame for my eternal distress. My mom thought it was mean. Thanks, Mom. At least I know you're on my side.

Truth is, even the two sticker villains were ultimately on my side. They knew I'd use it as incentive to heal, and I did. I was determined to do whatever it took to take that sticker off of the chair. I showed them.

Suzi and Catherine had a lot of similar traits. They were both observant and understanding. You know how some people just get it? They just get it. In my room was this awful painting done in creepy abstract colors of a cartoon elderly man with horrific eyes walking a dog, and Suzi and I would come up with nightmarish backstories that could've inspired the illustrator. We wondered what the hell it was doing in a place where children are already scared out of their minds, but we knew why it was there for us: it made us cry laughing.

Suzi still fulfilled all of her normal nurse duties, like checking my vitals and giving me medicine, but she always did it in a way that was delightfully distracting. She'd point at the picture while putting in IVs to tell me that if I didn't get medicine, I'd end up with his freaky eyes. While I was asleep or on drugs one day— probably both—she put a temporary butterfly tattoo on my stomach. It was glittery and bright pink, not my typical look, but she thought I'd rock it and had to try. While I was getting my blood drawn, she would even bring in various themed Band-Aids to cover the spot of the injection. I refused them at first, but she and my parents wouldn't let me go with the regular ones from then on out. In complete seriousness, she told me that she had stolen them from the brain cancer children and would be personally offended if I kept saying no to them. She is a remarkable woman.

The nurses had informed me that there was a top floor of the hospital that had fun arts-and-crafts-related supplies and said I should venture up there in the chair. I had little interest and imagined that I'd be too old for it; I figured it'd be a lot of effort to get me up there and that I'd be in a room with other sick children who probably also thought they were too old for it. I was totally wrong.

The room is ginormous. Suzi convinced me to go with her, and I'm glad I did. I'm sure the "convincing" was really just her telling me that we were going to go and me begrudgingly following along. I remember being shocked once we got off the elevator onto the floor. It was bright and inviting. She rolled me first past the closet of movies and TV shows that they had on DVD so I could bring something back to my room, and they had everything you could possibly imagine. I mean, it was all probably PG and PG-13, but twelve-year-old me was impressed by the selection.

I ended up choosing *Modern Family* because they had every season of it available and I figured I might be there awhile. I ended up watching every episode of *Modern Family*. I love *Modern Family*, I do, but you know the feeling of setting a song as your alarm clock and then shivering whenever it's played after that? Now when I flip through daytime TV and hear Eric Stonestreet scream "Mitchell," I feel like melting. It served as a good way to pass time, though, because I definitely didn't feel like I had watched hours of it by the time it was over. That's my excuse for this epic binge.

We continued onward on the floor until Suzi brought me to a deck outside of the building. I don't fully remember the view, but I remember the wind. It was that wind that I couldn't feel outside of my house when I was first put in the ambulance, and it was the wind that passed by me when I'd run a race. It had only been just over a week since I'd been exposed to the movement of air, yet I felt reborn. I felt it only on parts of my left side because my sensation was still lacking quite a bit, but I embraced it as much as I could. It was magical.

Suzi had brought along some nail polish, which I assumed came from the bags of cards and gifts that had been sent to me. She painted on an atrocious dark purple color that was a bit too spooky for my taste, but it was nice to be pampered a little. My nails had grown longer than I'd ever let them because I was a serious nail-biter, so they actually looked pretty nice. When some of the polish got on my skin, Suzi confessed that she wasn't the best nail painter, which prompted my dad to joke that he hoped she was better with needles when it came to precision.

My left arm started moving a bit whenever the wind would hit it, which I assumed was just spasming. When my dad made note of it, though, I realized that I could move it back and forth about an inch. This was spectacular. I mean, I was looking at my arm and moving it with my brain and spine all working right enough to do it. I was stunned and ready to capture whatever power the wind and the nail polish had that afternoon to use for the rest of my mobility. I went back to the room having breathed fresh air on my own, having moved my arm on my own, and having a killer manicure. What more could I ask for?

When I wasn't watching *Modern Family*, I was watching the monitor I was attached to. I tried to make sense of the numbers, but I don't think I ever figured any of them out. When some of them would fluctuate, I'd track the lows and the highs that they'd reach before returning to what they'd normally be. This was a painfully boring game I'd play, but it kept me busy.

The doctors from various departments would do "rounds" every morning. They'd come in, perform tests and ask me questions, then disappear. There were about four or five of them in every group, from four or five different areas of specialty that would bring their team in to assess me. Sometimes when they'd appear confused or make hypotheses about when or if I'd ever move again, I'd want to reassure them that my monitor numbers weren't moving around too much and that I was therefore fine. I never did because I couldn't gauge whether I'd get a laugh or concern that I'd make a joke of the seemingly likely possibility of my paralyzed future, but I totally regret not trying anyways.

Humor carried me through everything. I had to laugh and joke around. How dull would this story be if I didn't? Some of the best laughter came from my community. My parents and I read the cards that were sent to me all the time. There were moments early on when I'd be too emotionally and physically overwhelmed to read any, but after a few days at Tufts we started to read about twenty or so a day. Many of my cards contained letters that were written with so much love and compassion that we couldn't help but burst into tears reading them. These sorts of cards reminded me that hundreds of people were thinking of me and hoping for my recovery. I felt like like I had a community of Haley fans.

Some cards made my father and I laugh hysterically, though. There were many cards from church groups that sent their prayers and love. This was unlike anything I had ever encountered, because people I didn't know in the slightest were caring deeply about me. It was extremely empowering, and it felt fantastic to know how much love I was receiving. My dad and I made jokes about our uncertainty regarding whether I had ever stepped foot in a church when we'd read these, but it was still great to know I was thought about.

We ended up stacking the cards that said something along the lines of "I never really knew you that well..." and found it pretty amazing that so many people who claimed to hardly know me had some memory with me that they wrote about, or some hope for me to return to Falmouth. On the other hand, I had a card from Catherine that was totally not endearing and was covered in stickers and glitter pen smudges. Every card was unique, let's just say.

There was one that I remember my mom was hesitant to read to me. I told her to anyways, and it said that the person who wrote it was excited that I had gotten on the "A team" for soccer and that she was looking forward to playing with me. Looking back on it, my heart does break a bit to think about what continuing soccer would've been like. I enjoyed playing, and this was the first I had heard that I'd gotten on the A team after the tryouts, which had happened just before my injury. However, at the time, I just responded to it with a laugh and "Guess that's not happening." I don't know where my optimism came from necessarily, but it was all over the place.

To say I had a favorite card or letter would be impossible. There was one card, though, that made my day unlike any other. It was your basic get-well card except on the front of it, the person had drawn a chicken. Now, it was a very good drawing of a chicken. There was shading and cross-hatching involved, so this chicken was created by an artist. But why, I had to ask, a chicken? We made numerous speculations, including the chance that a chicken was some symbol for health or something, and my dad asked me a few times to make sure I hadn't had any chicken-related situations with the person. He'd often read a few cards, then lift the chicken one from the side of my bed again, which would bring back the same laughter we had the first time we decided to speculate about why I'd receive a chicken card. The letters from home were all moving, and this one was absolutely included.

The community was very involved, from my time at Maine Medical Center on. Just a few days after the injury, a gathering was organized at the middle school. There was a sea of green, spinal-cord-injury-awareness outfits and green ribbons, and some of my friends tell me that this is when they first started tying green ribbons around streetlamps and power poles in town. I've seen videos from this event where my closest friends were making cards, sending love, hugging each other, crying, and a combination of all of the above. Families I knew, families I didn't know, even my teachers were there to support me before I had any idea that they knew where I was. In my Spanish classroom, my teacher didn't let anyone sit in my seat for the rest of the year. Catherine told me that many students in all three classes in the middle school wore green from that day to the end of school. I maybe have one green shirt, so that was both wildly impressive and sweet to hear.

There was also news coverage of that day about me on the local news station. It's only about two minutes long and is mostly made up of pictures of me from my iPod Touch that my mom had released to the world that did not exclude selfies meant for myself and my camera roll only, but it was still informative. One portion of it focuses on Lila, a lifelong best friend of mine, as she is in tears while wishing for me to get better. I don't know if I'll ever be able to watch those few seconds without feeling deeply saddened.

I knew that I had to prove my community right. I had to show them that I was capable of taking their thoughts and prayers to eventually return. I had to take it all on. I had to take on the pain and the stress because I had a family far larger than I had ever imagined, and they wanted me home.

There were trials that tested both my will and my physical capabilities. A man brought a machine we called the "coughing device" into my room to try to get my airways to open up. It was hell.

The device attaches to your mouth like a mask and sucks air inward like a vacuum. You're supposed to cough into the mask, and all the mucus that has built up is supposed to release through the tube. It's gross. It's even grosser when you can't cough no matter how hard you try. Every time he'd hold the mask to my face, I'd let out a pathetic and painful attempt at a cough that only ever sounded like a quick wheezing. The man who administered it was truly its only redeeming quality, because he assured me that we'd try it only until it hurt too much and that we could just as easily try another day. I had to try many days, and I still couldn't really cough until a bit into my stay at Spaulding Rehabilitation Center, after I'd left Tufts. Every time, I just thought to myself how gross the machine was and how pathetic I was.

The thoughts became way more grim when I realized that the only thing that made the machine gross was that it was trying to take the Mucus & Co. that was still inside of me. I don't know if any of you have the luxury of never having seen a Mucinex commercial, but I can only think of the animated mucus guy when I think of mucus, and that's what I thought was clogging my throat. It was nasty.

While the coughing device was seeing little success, so were the continual MRIs and tests I had to go through. I ended up having five

MRIs when all was said and done, each one as delightful as the last. There were some X-rays and other tests, but those were far less invasive. One time they had to put the jelly stuff on my chest for an ultrasound. I had never heard of an ultrasound being used for anything but pregnancy, so that was mildly concerning. The show *Jane the Virgin* hadn't come out yet and I'm glad, because I probably would have been way more freaked out. The MRIs were really the irritating tests. None of them were as long as the five-and-a-half-hour one I had at Maine Med, but they were always uncomfortable and long. They also never seemed to do much when it came to determining what had happened to me.

The doctors not knowing what had happened was exactly as alarming as it sounds. I was naïve, so to me, not knowing a cause equaled their not having any idea how to help me heal. They did draw a lot of conclusions, though. Doctors have to be super clear about things to patients and their families, and they didn't seem too afraid to tell me that the likelihood of my ever moving my right side again was slim. With that came the idea that I'd never walk again, or eat by myself again, or breathe on my own again, etc., etc. I one hundred percent respect doctors because they do fantastic things when they're right, but here they were wrong in the greatest way.

They would give me injections at night to try to speed my recovery. I don't know what they were for; I just know that I needed one every night on the sides of my stomach. Now, I had seen the tattoo pain scale images, so I knew that the side of my stomach was not going to be a comfortable place to insert a needle beneath my skin, but alas, these things were out of my control. I had one every night, alternating sides. This was until I started regaining sensation on the right side of my chest. Turns out, if you stick a giant needle into a hypersensitive part of your body, it will be the most painful thing you've ever experienced. From then on we did it only on the left, and it felt like nothing in comparison.

When I FaceTimed my friend Ike for the first time, I don't know which was redder—the blood circulating through my IV tubes or my blushing face. I could hardly speak, but Ike seemed unbelievably excited to hear my whisper-like voice. I remember peering down into the bottom right corner of the screen to look at myself once or twice during the call, and although I distinctly recall having as many chins as a classic dad selfie, I was able to see myself next to him, and God, was that comforting.

I technically started physical therapy at Tufts, although I could never really handle more than about five minutes of it before whatever limbs could move got tired. My lungs weren't yet strong enough for speech therapy beyond practicing breath control and trying to sustain minimal conversations, and I wasn't showing signs of fine-motor skill improvement, so there was no occupational therapy yet either. Even though I was making strides at incredible rates, there was still a hell of a long way to go to get to where I am now. The best part about recovery at this stage was the uncertainty, though. I had no way of telling how far I'd go. I was told I wouldn't breathe on my own, talk at a normal volume, walk on my own, or move my right side at all. I'm glad I learned not to listen to people who told me I couldn't do something.

Two young nurses came into my room to talk to me about the concept of physical therapy for the gross-motor movement I was starting to exhibit. They began raising my bed by using a little button on the side, which hurt more than it ever had. In an only sort of emo way, the pain was brilliant. The pain meant sensation was flowing back into my nerves. So even though having my back moved upward by recliner felt like I was being stabbed, I was recovering.

When I was lifted up to look at them, my eyes very quickly met the rest of my body, which I hadn't really seen much of recently. It was thinner than ever, colorless, and veiny. After surveying the uncomfortable sight of my own poked and prodded limbs, I eventually looked back up at the two women.

They lifted my arms and asked me to move them as much as I could. I was able to push my left arm inward with assistance, but that was about it. I also hated the feeling of displacing my arm from its resting position because I knew I wouldn't be able to put it back once I did. It sounds a little obsessive, but moving my arm out of a place that was comfortable was frightening, even if I knew someone would reset it if I asked.

Once they realized there was little to work with, they moved to my legs. As they put their arms around my calves, I noticed the bear-like leg hair that had accumulated in the previous eleven days. In a sad attempt to normalize the situation, I jokingly apologized for the appalling lengths to which my Italian hair had grown. They laughed it off and told me not to worry, then continued with their exam.

I could kick my left leg quite a bit, but I couldn't control how high or the direction in which it would fling up into the air. My right leg was refusing to move at all. The two nurses informed me that they would have to discuss the results of their tests before I could actually do any sort of therapy, but that they could let me know as soon as they had any sort of answers. They reemerged from behind the plastic curtains in front of my door in just minutes. The shorter of the two told me in a painfully slow and depressed voice that they didn't think physical therapy would be beneficial yet. The other was quick to interrupt her.

She didn't disagree with the therapy analysis, but she did offer something else that could help with my healing. She said that they had razors and could help me shave my legs if I wanted them to.

Okay, so let's break this down. I couldn't move enough to even work on moving, which felt a little pathetic. I had been a running, self-shaving twelve-year-old, and now I was being told that it was too soon to start physical therapy. However, there was an alternative! I could have my legs shaved by these two nurses to try to make up for any sadness associated with that reality. Great. Awesome. Shaving and trying to break through paralysis were being given the same level of importance in my life.

So yeah, of course I said yes. Not unlike the hosts of TLC's *What Not to Wear*, the two seemed thrilled that I had accepted their offer of a mini transformation. When they brought out the fresh, disposable razors, I was actually excited. It was just another thing that mimicked "normal" life for a girl my age, and I was all for it. That is, until they started.

When they shaved my legs, I felt like they were taking an X-Acto knife to my skin. It was awful. I had been through a lot on the pain scale over my time at Tufts, and this definitely reached the top. Again, the pain was a good thing because pain=feeling, but it hurt like a bitch. Luckily, it hurt like a bitch on both of my legs. The right side of my body was catching up to my left, which meant recovery. I let them get everywhere below the knees as if I always shaved only beneath my knees, but my jaw hurt from how tightly I was clenching my teeth to keep the pain hidden. I wasn't going to let the pain stop me from having a moment of normality. Shaving still hurts pretty intensely to this day. My left leg feels totally fine, but the feeling in my right still resembles this agony. If you see me wearing jeans in the summertime, you know why.

In my last few days at Tufts, Suzi was almost always my nurse. She admitted to me once that she agreed to work one day only if she could be with me, which made me overwhelmingly jazzed as it exploded my ego. Sometimes she'd come in, give me a shot of some sort, then just sit with me and talk about life and middle school and boys. By the end of our gossip, she was determined to set me up with one of my best friends. Sometimes she'd just wash and brush my hair so self-care didn't have to be limited to uncomfortable towel washes in bed. The fact that I was twelve, exhausted, and hardly moving, eating, or talking was forgotten every time we'd "hang out." It was weirdly empowering.

I hadn't yet done much for speech therapy, but talking to her became easier as my breathing improved. The laughter hurt during the feeding-tube era, but once that was removed, laughter felt warm and helpful. I knew I loved the sensation of laughter most when another one of my nurses revealed that Suzi had been on an episode of *Family Feud*. After that glittery butterfly tattoo, you can bet I was going to find the footage.

As soon as I was able to locate the video on Google, I showed my parents and every nurse on the floor. Apparently some of the nurses dropped hints that they had seen it when Suzi's next shift began, because she pretty immediately came into my room with an accusatory look on her face. I was getting ready to transfer out of the PICU at Tufts into Spaulding Rehabilitation Center by this point, and I think we both shared a moment of sadness because our pranks would come to an end. Of course, the sadness was only a short-lived piece of the emotions we were both experiencing. Spaulding meant a new age. Spaulding was the

next step in finding myself again, and Nurse
Suzi and I couldn't have been more excited for
this upgrade.

We were set to leave the following
morning. This was the first night my nurses
offered a cannula instead of a BiPAP machine
to help me breathe at night. The BiPAP
machine is commonly used for people with
insomnia or other sleeping problems, but I don't
think anyone would ever use this contraption of
their own free will. It's a large mask that
suctions to your face and provides pure oxygen
to support lung functioning. A strap would be
tightly strapped around my ears, and by
morning my face muscles and earlobes would
ache with sharp pain. This night was going to
be different.

The cannula is a far less cruel device. It's
a little tube that also releases oxygen, like a
BiPAP, but in a much nicer fashion. It rests
gently beneath your nostrils and pushes air
upward into them. It wraps around your ears,
but you hardly feel anything. The cannula is
like the oxygen device that would use good

manners and ask you how you're doing after you miss a day of school. I recognize that I'm personifying a cannula, but really, it deserves this kind of an explanation. Sleeping was much easier, and I kept it on for most of the day, too, just to make the rest of the day a little simpler when it came to breathing. Only about a day later, I didn't need anything to support my breathing anymore.

Quick side note because we're on the topic of breathing: Please don't smoke. Please. I cannot express to you how difficult it is to breathe when your lungs aren't working all that well, and I can only imagine that lung cancer would be way worse. Thank you.

Anyways, breathing on my own was also accompanied by the removal of all the IVs and wires that were still attached to me. I still needed the monitor to track my breathing, but I was pretty much ready to go recover in a rehab facility instead of an ICU. This was a day that at the beginning of Tufts I can confidently say we weren't sure would come, but every day saw progress, and I was finally ready to move on. Thank. God.

By the next morning I was off. I was wheeled out of Tufts on a gurney with my parents by my side, eager to enter the unknown. As we were leaving the floor and going toward the elevator, a loud male voice echoed down the hallway behind us. We stopped and turned to see my head doctor racing to catch us before we left. He wished me good luck and said goodbye to my family and me. This moment accurately defined my experience with the entire staff at Tufts. They were all phenomenal, and they all wanted me the hell out of there so I could continue on.

Spaulding

Spaulding was absolutely stunning. The entire facility was new, because it had opened up in April 2013, just after the Boston bombing. The place had everything you could ever need while trying to regain movement. There was a kitchen on the floor with a giant gym that had entirely handicapped-accessible, adjustable cabinets and sinks. There was a car seat with pedals at the bottom in the gym, but I was too young to drive at this point, so I never really spent much time by it. The gym was huge, bright, and always buzzing with physical and occupational therapists with their patients. Wires fell from the ceiling that could suspend new walkers in the air for standing practice, and high-tech machines and pieces of exercise equipment were everywhere.

The pediatric unit was on the top floor at Spaulding, which gave us unmatched views of Boston Harbor and the city skyline. The room was far more luxurious than I had imagined, and the bathroom attached to the room was large and close by. At night, my bed was positioned in such a way that I was staring out toward the glowing city lights of Boston. My parents and I often joked that Spaulding would be a five-star hotel if you didn't get entry by being injured.

Furthermore, at the end of the hallways were these communal spaces called "lantern rooms." The name makes complete sense when you see it because it is almost entirely windows and you can see everything from Logan Airport to the Citgo sign they always focus on during Red Sox games. Below, one could see a playground full of children and families from the early mornings onward throughout the day. Children in wheelchairs would race up and down its open concept design, and I'd sit in awe at the hugeness of it all. I remember wondering about the children who looked down upon this playground during the wintertime when it was closed off. I remember wondering about the children who were here during the holidays.

My very first day at Spaulding was not ideal.
Within just a few minutes of arriving, I was
visited by my friend Grace F. and her family.
Grace is the girl I had always aspired to be like.
I mean, she was bright, charming, and
indescribably kind. I was nervous about seeing
her because I figured she'd be put off by my
new look. However, when she walked into the
room I had only just adjusted to, she greeted me
with familiar and energized eyes. My heart
swelled with excitement because I felt like I
was reconnecting with someone who
represented everything I wanted to be like...
Then I pissed myself.

I never thought this story would be
funny, but I think of it and chuckle
occasionally. You see, I still had very little
function in the majority of my body by the time
of Spaulding, and I certainly didn't have any
control over anything from my waist down. So,
things happen. I'm stunned that I've reached the
point where I can be at peace with that
statement, but I truly believe that sometimes
things just happen, maybe without reason.

During my time at Tufts, I had gotten pretty comfortable with the state of my body. I knew that what I could and could not do was not in my control yet. Nonetheless, I was mortified. Seeing someone who reminds you of beauty and goodness like Grace did and then watching yourself exhibit a less-than-beautiful display was a bitter and painful contrast.

I played it off as needing a moment with a nurse and the situation was quickly resolved, but it was a depressing way to begin my stay at Spaulding—a place where I was supposed to start gaining this kind of mobility and control. The rest of the visit was wonderful, and I fondly remember Grace turning these dark thoughts upside down during her time there with her family. She even brought me Victoria's Secret shampoo and conditioner, which I continued to purchase and use for an upsettingly long time afterward. Her presence and this little gesture transformed a day that could have been defined by a humiliating accident into one that will be thought of in a positive and grateful light.

After Grace left, I started to meet the nursing staff. They were all incredibly friendly, but I did miss Suzi quite a bit. I was in the room closest to the front-desk area because I was in pretty critical condition despite being transferred over from Tufts. My breathing was still lacking and I still had to be connected to a monitor whenever I wasn't in the bathroom. This all changed rather rapidly.

My therapy schedules were pretty rigorous, considering the fact that the last time I had tried physical therapy, I'd just ended up with partially shaved legs. I had to do physical therapy for gross-motor movement, and occupational for my hands. These both started in my room, but I eventually graduated into the gym and another side room on the floor throughout the fifty or so days I was there. I even did some speech therapy for a little while to practice breathing and talking at the same time—an unheard-of concept, really. But none of this could commence before I sat up in bed first.

Sitting up in bed was going to be the beginning of the last major leg of my recovery. My work at Spaulding would truly begin the very first time I tried to sit up. We began by using the buttons on my bed to slowly elevate me into an upright position, which hurt tremendously. Of course, the pain was so severe because so much of my sensation was starting to come back. I was feeling pain everywhere on my left side and parts of my right. I kinda loved it.

Sitting up was very difficult for a long time. Like just about everything, though, I eventually got the hang of it. Once I could balance myself, it was determined that my core muscles were strong enough for physical therapy. I met my physical therapist that same day.

Krista was young, talkative, and a perfect match for me. She talked me through everything before we'd ever try anything new, but she also pushed me to take on challenges I didn't think I'd be able to start. We ran into many setbacks along the way, but we persevered as a team through it all.

Before we could do much of anything else, we had to make sure I wouldn't get light-headed while sitting or standing up for long periods of time. This was wildly frustrating because I had no control over how dizzy I'd get, and the paleness of my face made trying to pretend I wasn't dizzy pretty impossible. In order to get my body used to this sort of position, I was strapped onto a machine that would slowly go from a horizontal to a vertical position with the touch of a button.

The machine screamed medieval torture more than any other one had, and it sort of reminded me of the kind of board that magicians' assistants are tied to when knives are thrown at them. There were no knives involved—in fact I don't really remember much pain being involved either—but it still wasn't pleasant.

We had to time ourselves when I'd get into the vertical position to see how long it took before I'd be overcome with queasiness, and after a while this became very boring. So, Krista brought along Hedbanz.

The game of Hedbanz requires you to put on a plastic headband with a cardholder, and insert a random card from a stack. The card has a noun on it, and you have to try to figure out what word is on your forehead by asking only yes or no questions. My dad, Krista, and I played Hedbanz like it was nobody's business. We became super competitive and invested, which meant we were able to spend less and less time focusing on my blood pressure.

By the last time I was strapped into the machine, we were top-notch Hedbanz opponents. My dad had the word *zebra* on his forehead, and I was determined to figure out my card before he figured out his. Turns out, when *waffle* is on your forehead and *zebra* is on your opponent's, it is difficult to figure them out even with mastery-level skill. We spent about twenty minutes going back and forth until I realized my word. Not only had I just won the game, but I had also been upright without feeling dizzy for our goal amount of time. Two points to Haley that afternoon.

Getting up in bed was no longer a challenge, and I used their standard wheelchairs to get to and from therapy. Krista introduced me to the hanging wires in the gym, which we used to hoist me up while she and my parents would move my legs as though I were walking. We brought out mirrors so I could see my progress without having to move in uncomfortable ways, and I was able to watch my right leg kick for the first time. After the kick, we were ready to move forward in terms of walking. Krista put tape on the floor in a straight line and, with her support, I began trying to walk with one foot on each side of it. This was a bold step and it was very unsuccessful initially, but after about ten days I was walking the stretch on the hallway while keeping my feet apart.

Soon after the walking process began, Krista introduced me to the Lokomat, a device that straps in each of your limbs and moves each one for you as if you are standing and walking. The machine resembled the gym equipment in my basement that I had never bothered figuring out how to use. I was put into it a few times, and although the plastic straps gave me bruises, it did feel like normal walking for the most part.

Shortly thereafter, I was getting the hang of taking a few steps to the couch in my room and back to my bed. Walking was freeing, even if I could sustain it for only three or four steps. My left leg was strengthening quickly. I wanted to start doing things on my own.

I was still being assisted with most daily activities, but I desperately wanted to prove that I didn't need help anymore. Truth is, I did still need help; I was just eager to move on. So, I proposed the notion of being able to use the restroom on my own without a nurse. I was shot down before I could get too excited about it.

Not long afterward, Krista granted me this privilege. I still needed help showering until the last few days of my stay at Spaulding, but even that became easier with practice. My occupational therapy had come along enough by the end for me to finally open shampoo bottles and bathe myself, too. It was a heroic feeling, but none of it came quickly or easily.

Occupational therapy was always more upsetting than physical therapy. I had a great therapist and a good plan for how we'd move forward, but starting to walk versus staring at your fingers and trying to move them with your mind is an unfair comparison. A lot of occupational therapy included pinching putty with various thicknesses and degrees of resistance. Sometimes they had me practice handwriting with a pencil lodged between my stiff and unresponsive left-hand fingers. Four years of experience writing with my left hand and I still can hardly manage a paragraph before my fingers give in. I still identify as a righty, because let me tell you, the left-hand world is cruel, and I did not know my privilege until it was lost.

My friend Sarah N. joined me once for occupational therapy, and we ended up moving to a different floor where there was a kitchen and baking supplies. I loved baking and decorating before my injury, and although using a Betty Crocker just-add-oil mix wasn't the same, it was close. We practiced opening the boxes with my right hand, failing, then trying with my left. We did the same with cracking eggs, stirring ingredients, and various other tasks. That was occupational therapy. It was slow.

Speech therapy was never something I spent long doing. There was this tube that I had to blow into for the first few days at Spaulding that measured how much air I was able to release. Similar to those carnival stands that charming boyfriends always whack with a hammer to get the girl a stuffed animal and show off their strength in movies, the little measuring piece of plastic would shoot up as you breathe, then fall back down. We did this a few times a day until my talking and breath control was relatively normal again. I had hardly been able to talk by the end of my stay at Tufts, but my speaking became relatively normal within a few days of my arrival at Spaulding. The most productive speech therapy was practicing accents with my dad and joking around, if you ask me.

I'm going to break up the chronology a bit and compile the rest of my visits with people at Spaulding into the next section because I figure those will make the most sense together.

Sophie G. was the first visitor I remember well aside from Grace. I was looking forward to seeing Sophie because she and I have always been a power duo and I adored joking around with her in classes and in clubs and sports we were involved in. She came to visit with her mother, whom I had also known well before May, and it was honestly just delightful to see them both. I had my nurses comb my hair and put me in athletic shorts and my nicest T-shirt so that they'd see me in my best state, but I still think I was a bit shocking.

Sophie seemed rather tense for most of the visit. She certainly appeared loving and excited, but there was a very apparent hesitation in the way she spoke. That made sense to me. She had only ever known me to be loud and mobile and I was neither of those things anymore, but I couldn't help but wonder if she'd always be this way around me from here on out. At the end of the visit, we had a few moments alone when my parents were in the room telling the details of my story to her mother while we were outside, and I remember making a stroke joke to lighten the mood.

I couldn't possibly tell you what the joke was. I'm sure it was crude and offensive, probably insanely self-deprecating, but I figured it might break the ice that had frozen between us. I think there was a quick pause but so quick that I can't remember it enough to be sure. We laughed hysterically. We were off and running. I was reuniting my old self with her while incorporating my new circumstances. I was proving to someone that I really was the same person inside, and it was unbelievably refreshing. Sophie and I now do debate, theatre, and various other activities together with a bond far stronger than one that would probably have emerged before my injury and this visit.

I was visited a few days later by one of my former softball coaches, Coach Carlisle. He brought food, which was greatly appreciated because even though things didn't taste like metal anymore, they did still taste like hospital. He also brought with him a little figurine-like beach set. Written on the top was "a day at the beach," which he said he brought along because it appeared I wouldn't get one of those that summer. It was a small gesture that meant so much. In my mind, the beach kit symbolized a family that was thinking of my situation and wanting the best for me all the way through it, and that wanted me to escape it as soon as I could.

My parents gave him the story and I filled in spots here and there, but what I remember most about this visit was, weirdly enough, his voice. I had only really spoken to him in the softball setting, where he'd yell out praise or tips when I was pitching on the mound during games. Not once during the meeting did he turn his voice into anything more high-pitched or less genuine than I was used to on the field. He still just seemed like my coach, except this time instead of pitching well, I was standing and walking.

Catherine came to visit with some other friends of mine, and she had an interesting perspective, because even though I hadn't really felt like I was progressing all that much, she noted a significant difference between what I looked like now versus Tufts. I showed her the lantern room and we wheeled around for a bit; this time I knew that if she tried to put a sticker on my chair, I'd remove it with ease.

After Catherine came by, my friend Jessica visited. Jessica and her family were watching my devilish cat for the time that I was away, so many of my initial questions for her were about how he was doing. She showed me pictures of him and laughed along to stories about his interactions with her German shepherd puppy.

She also brought along a bunch of One Direction magazines. We cut out the posters from them and hung them all over my room. I was obsessed with Louis Tomlinson, a member of the band, so much that my kitten was named after him. She taped them all over my walls and totally transformed my room into a Haley-themed museum. Her energy and excitement brought the teenage spirit I had lost into my life again. We gossiped about the drama I had missed, school, the totally surreal fact that my crush had been wearing green every day. We just enjoyed each other's company as though it were a sleepover. That one visit inspired me to get home like none of the others because I felt so utterly ready to reenter life as a stronger, wiser version of myself. Although I felt super on top of the world after this reunion, I did still fear seeing some of the people from my life beforehand.

When my first major crush-turned-best-friend Ike was coming down to visit, I was overcome with anxiety. This wasn't the anxiety that accompanies a math test or getting on a plane, but rather the nervous energy that comes with Christmas Eve or the night before a birthday. I had no feelings for Ike in any way beyond our strong friendship, but I still wanted him to see me in the best way possible. I wanted him to look at me and know that I was doing well, that I missed and loved him infinitely. So, I took the only logical next step. I scheduled an appointment with one of my nurses to braid my hair before he arrived.

One of my nurses ended up taking about forty-five minutes out of her day to French braid my hair, and I felt so much more put together. I knew that an oversized T-shirt, gym shorts, unshaven legs, a drooping right eye, and messy hair wouldn't look "pretty," so I just got rid of the messy hair part. This made probably zero difference when it came to what I looked like in the eyes of someone who hadn't seen me in a while, but it made all the difference for my confidence.

When Ike and his mom came through the door, all of my nervousness vanished. I was up in a wheelchair because that was the most progressed version of myself that I could show them, and I felt an instant warmth accompanying their presence. Ike brought me the essentials: a pair of Red Sox sweatpants that I still wear to rehearsals every now and again, lime-green nail polish, a rubber duck, and a bike horn to put on my wheelchair. The lime-green nail polish was not really my style, but after the witch-like purple from Tufts, I was willing to experiment. These little gifts brought him into my everyday life at Spaulding for the rest of my time there. I texted him on the daily, but I now had tangible reminders of his love. While texting that night, we talked about what the future would look like. I remember being pretty much clueless. Then, he sent me a link to a YouTube video.

The video was a clip from *Santa Claus is Comin' to Town!* where the characters sing, "Put one foot in front of the other, and soon you'll be walking out the door." I rolled my eyes when it got to this chorus, but my parents laughed for days about it. If only it were that simple. By the time I was walking, my dad

constantly brought up this text to my therapists.
Okay, fine, I guess it was kinda funny.

Before Ike left, he told me all about how
his baseball team had my "Stark" jersey in their
dugouts during games. My coach from when I
first started softball was their current coach, the
one who visited me at Maine Medical Center,
and he had apparently told the team that "we
carry baseball bags, and she's carrying IV
ones."

It was unreal to see photos of the team
with green ribbons and immense support. I
knew them all, but had never known them all
that well. I felt like I was at their games with
them in a sense. I hope they felt that way too.
Perhaps this feeling was what inspired me to
drive over eight hours to surprise them at their
game in Connecticut after I got home.

The team was doing so well that they
ended up playing on ESPN during the daytime.
I had been home for only a few weeks when
Delaney and I figured we could make their
game in the afternoon if we left early in the

morning. My mom was on board without a second thought, and we gathered materials to make posters for them.

When I showed up, I was still walking with a walker. As soon as we parked outside the field, I sent Ike a "Good luck, I have therapy so I won't be able to watch your game but I'm recording it!" text. Sike. That's what he gets for "one foot in front of the other."

It took a while to climb all the steps to get onto the bleachers, but when I turned the corner at the top, I was met with unexpected applause and a standing ovation from the team's families. My mom went down to inform Coach Rogers of my arrival, and within seconds the entire team stopped getting ready so they could come up and hug or fist-bump me. Seeing all the boys at once so eager to see me was amazing. All this time I'd been certain I was behind them, supporting them through their games, they were doing the same for me.

My next visit at Spaulding was with Olivia. Olivia and I spent a few hours together, but there was one point in particular that I'll remember forever. We sat outside the hospital and had a discussion about how people were reacting to my injury. The conversation was deeply personal and I plan to keep the details confidential, but she provided a new insight into how it was really affecting people in a greatly emotional way. I had ignorantly assumed that only my closest friends would have these sorts of responses, but I found out that the sadness was nonexclusive. The care I was being given was not confined to my inner circle, my family, or my nurses. I was cared about by everyone.

Delaney's visit is the last individual one I'll mention for the sake of continuing my story, but this one is far too important to exclude. By the time I saw Delaney, I was getting around in my wheelchair pretty well. I gave her a tour of the facility, and we stopped at the rooftop garden not far from the gym to take a picture. It was then that I decided I would show off a little.

When my mom pulled up her phone to take the picture, I tried to stand up. Surprisingly, I did it. I was a bit leaned over and could manage to stay upright for only a few seconds, but I had my arm around one of my best friends and was feeling more camera-ready than ever before. I went from "Delaney's friend" who could run fast during indoor track to Delaney's friend who was using a wheelchair to Delaney's friend who could stand up to have her picture taken. Delaney was a witness to one of the most major milestones in my stay at Spaulding, and there's no one else I can imagine having that moment with.

All of my visits at Spaulding were life altering in some way, and I had so many that I've included only these few. Know that if you did visit me and I didn't write about it, I do remember and appreciate the time we shared. I'd also love to talk about our experience anytime. It's also important to note that even though I felt as though I could pour my heart and soul into this book with just about everything that happened, my visit with Lila is one that I cannot describe. I don't have the words to convey the specialness of that reunion, and although they may come with time, that visit deserves a way with words that I don't possess yet.

After countless visits, perhaps the most highly awaited one was approaching. It had been on my calendar for a while, and I waited impatiently, as it felt like eons before we X'd through the last day before this one. I wanted it to be perfect.

I was very much looking forward to going to see *The Fault in Our Stars* for a few reasons. First, my dad had been reading the book to me at nights and we had finished it as the movie was being released. Also, it was about a girl who was a teenager going through medical nightmares, and I found a lot of it to be pretty relatable. My friends were driving to the AMC Theatre near my hospital where I would meet them, and I was very excited. I had been at Spaulding for almost three weeks, and I desperately wanted a little escape.

When we arrived, I had some difficulty getting from our car seat to the wheelchair, but we managed. The theatre was huge and wheelchair accessible so there was no trouble getting me and my clan inside. They all wore green, and it was indescribably fun to feel like I was just out and about with a group of my friends again.

We posed in front of the picture of Ansel Elgort outside the theatre for a photo that has pretty powerful hidden meanings. I'm smiling in this photo, which is probably because I'm outside with wind and friends, and I'm sitting upright in my chair. My left hand is wide open, pretending to caress Ansel's hair, so my left hand was almost completely moving and feeling at this point. My friends are standing with their hands over various parts of Ansel as well, so this picture is a perfect reminder that despite everything we were all going through, we were still the fun-loving, tween girls we'd been when I left town.

I don't know if this group of friends remembers what happened after the movie was over, but unfortunately I associate these last few moments with the day just about every time it crosses my mind. After the movie was through,

I tried to move from my seat back into my wheelchair. I'd been unwilling to sit in the handicap seats, so my mom had helped me up into one of the recliners so that I could sit with all my friends. When we tried to get back down the stairs, we were less successful.

I fell down, and even though my mom immediately tried to help me back up, I was sobbing by the time she had her arms around me again. I believe I got back up quickly and got into my chair, but that moment lasts an eternity in my memory. I was so embarrassed and disappointed that it took a great deal of distraction to pretend as though I wasn't upset about what had happened for the rest of the afternoon. My friends were a phenomenal distraction and none of them seemed to change how they acted because of it, which I was thankful for, but it still hurt. I had assumed that nothing would go wrong, and that was my first mistake. My friends really did handle it well. None of them seemed fazed by it, and although I was internally mortified, none of that horror was coming from external sources.

Maintaining whatever sense of dignity I had left after my first "shower" back at Tufts was always a difficult task. It was never easy to pretend that moving so little of my body wasn't insanely uncomfortable. If I could do it all over, I'd ignore my persistent desire to hold on to the abstract concept of dignity and just let myself heal in the awkward fashion that would occur.

The greatest test of my dignity was surprisingly not the showers or the baths by the time I'd gotten to Spaulding. I had become very aware and accepting of the necessity for hygiene and my inability to tend to it myself. Even writing this book I never really got too nervous about exposing the truth about hygiene for the injured. The biggest emotional challenge came with finding a wheelchair I could use in the gym.

There was a bright red chair that seemed to fit me best, and I was not excited about it. It wasn't the brightness or the redness that turned me off; red happens to be my favorite color and is the color of my current Subaru. The concept of getting fitted for a wheelchair was the difficult part.

There was something so overwhelmingly semi-permanent about it. I'm unbelievably grateful that this wheelchair wasn't something I'd have to live with forever, even though I didn't know that at the time. Nonetheless, it was symbolic of a lot of time ahead of me where I'd be using it instead of a walker. It was better than the temporary chairs in the sense that I could use it whenever my parents wanted to take me on walks inside or around the building, but it was still a bittersweet acceptance.

A few days later, I was wheeling myself slowly but surely around the floor. I wore a glove on my left hand, and the force I could exert out of my arm was just enough to keep the wheels turning. I'm surprised I didn't have a super-buff left arm at any point, because it felt like I was working it out all day long, more so than I ever had in sports.

We got pretty good use of the chair. Both of my parents wheeled me a few blocks away from the hospital every now and again to visit a market nearby. The market was my favorite place to be because the market meant I could buy real-people food. By "real-people food" I don't mean fresh cooked meals. I mean Pringles, Chex Mix, Peanut Butter M&Ms, and any variety of gorgeously processed salty foods I could want. I felt like a kid walking into the Wonka factory every time I went in there. I was raised on Kraft mac-and-cheese, and I missed those familiar tastes.

The hospital food at Spaulding was honestly pretty great. I really can't complain much about it; I was far more focused on the fact that my parents made me use my hardly moving hands to eat than the food itself. At Tufts I imagine the food was just as satisfactory. I just have no way of telling because of my metal flavoring medicine. I must admit, though, that when we found a calzone place that delivered to Spaulding, there was no turning back.

I ate entire pepperoni calzones on an every-other-night basis. They were large and greasy and definitely not super healthy, but I think my parents and doctors were okay with a carb overload after all the weight I had lost. It's way more concerning when I have calzone binges now than when I was having them back then.

After I had gained a new sense of freedom in the wheelchair, I made it a point to roam around and explore. One afternoon while wheeling around, I decided to take a pit stop in the child life room. There were two young siblings, probably about six or seven years old, playing Wii Sports on the TV. One was a girl in a wheelchair who appeared to move her arms well. She had big curly hair tied in scrunchies of various colors. The other was a boy leaning on the wheels next to her with very similar hair. I approached them and told them how much my brother and I used to love playing that game. That made the girl smile, even though she was clearly a bit shy. I didn't want to pry, so I planned to turn around. Then, the boy introduced them.

His name was Samuel and hers was Shayna. They had been to Spaulding before for various other reasons, but not for a while. Sam did most of the talking for his sister, but she eventually interrupted him and asked if I could play a round of Wii tennis with her. I was unsure if I'd be able to, but I figured that if I couldn't, she would probably not be able to tell the difference. She seemed upset by her brother's victory in the last match, so my hand injury was actually quite helpful when it came to the task of making sure she'd win.

She did, and just as the game was over, her mother walked into the room. This woman was put together but had already acquired the exhausted eyes I noticed all around the floor. She introduced herself to me, and we talked a bit about the injuries that had brought us together in this moment. It felt like we shared telepathic communication beneath the words we were saying, a secret, impossible-to-describe language that conveyed our heartbreak about being on that floor.

I began becoming more talkative with some of the families on the floor. I met a young girl, probably seven or eight, named Brooke who had sisters who stayed by her side through all her time in the hospital. She was the sweetest, happiest girl you'd ever see, with two big braces up her legs and a wheelchair. Despite her apparent happiness, I couldn't help but feel crushed.

I wanted to take it for her. From the second she flashed me her smile, I wanted to take it all for her. There was a pain in my chest that felt like it was choking me, not unlike when fluids were drained from my lungs at Tufts. I felt uneasy, faint, and wrong to be sad about having one brace when she wheeled around with two. All I could offer her family was love and understanding, but I was determined to do that as much as I could even with my own tight schedule. By the time I left, she had handwritten three cards to my parents and me. I have no more valuable a possession.

I became close with a young boy named Braydon and his mother as well. All the nurses talked about Braydon because of his intelligence and extroversion. We spent a lot of time talking because his grasp of life and the importance he placed on love and happiness was fascinating. I have never met a kid so young with so much poise, understanding, and compassion. He knew facts about things I'd never learned in school, and he knew something about every single nurse and doctor he had met. I felt as though every time I spoke to him, I was being exposed to a mind-set that I couldn't have ever achieved on my own. Braydon is one of the most special human beings I will ever encounter in my lifetime. When I think about whether I was chosen to have this injury because something knew I could take it on, I'm sure something knew that Braydon could take on his.

If I can tell you anything about being on the pediatric floor at Spaulding, it's that every kid there is incredibly strong. Every single family that goes through that facility is strong. These sick children are not all depressed and hopeless—no, they are quite the opposite. These children are fighters and they are happy and they are battling with hearts that have barely been given time to develop. They have a knowledge of the world that is beyond imagination, and I will forever respect these kids and the countless others in similar positions. They are warriors.

On the first floor of Spaulding is a giant, totally accessible pool room for "aquatic therapy." Although I never really knew how to swim well before my injury, Krista assured me that all I'd really have to be able to do is stand up. I was never keen on the idea, but the therapists I'd have would suggest it on a daily basis, and by the time we ended up trying it out, I think I was grateful for the little change of pace.

When the day actually arrived for us to go use the pool, I was less than accepting of the concept. I knew from the moment the idea sprouted in my therapists' minds that I would not be putting on a bathing suit. I was hardly able to look at my body in the shower, and I was certainly not ready to reveal it to the world. I live in a house with a pool and a hot tub now, and I still rarely go in either without a shirt and gym shorts. I can understand how this would make me seem pretty insecure, but I'm still immature enough to appreciate when clothing inflates with water underneath it, so I don't plan to change my mentality anytime soon.

Aside from the bathing suit, I was still generally pessimistic about it. I knew that if the pool water were slightly too hot or cold, my right side would spasm, and I was making progress in my regular therapy that I didn't want to halt.

I tried it anyways. At this point, the amount of unheard-of circumstances that had found their way into my life made me pretty certain that I could try just about anything once and be fine. When we got to the pool, it took us quite a while to actually get me inside of it.

There were stairs that could bring you in as well as a machine that lowered a type of wheelchair that could get wet. I took the stairs route, which was probably the most challenging part of the hour. It was lukewarm on my left but scorching on my right. Figures. Once I was submerged, we practiced kicks with both legs and very basic resistance training against the water. I got used to the temperature difference after a little while and could see how this might be nice for people who had swum before their injury, but it just wasn't for me. I also had a bit of a fear of water in general because of my lack of mobility, but that wasn't really much of an issue here. No, that was way more prevalent when they got me into a canoe in the harbor a few days later.

Yep, you read that right. I'm terrified of bodies of water. I mean, I'm sure the fear is more of drowning than of the water, but the two go hand in hand. When two young therapists I hadn't met before proposed the idea of riding in a canoe, I declined without a second thought. Then I heard Braydon excitedly agreeing to the offer with his mom. If Braydon could do it, I could do it. Besides, fear is so limiting. I'm afraid of drowning, but I've never really come close. I wasn't afraid of having a stroke and then that came out of nowhere, so maybe the unpredictability of life is the most compelling argument against fear.

The canoe ride was actually really fun. I know I just went on a tangent about how I was overcoming my fears and such, but every time we tipped a little, I still got the heebie-jeebies. Mind over matter, right?

We ended up rowing all over the harbor outside the playground area. My arms grew weak quickly, so I ended up just moving my oars in the motion with everyone else, even though I wasn't really adding any force whatsoever; I was like the person in every group project who signed their name at the top even though they most certainly did not uphold their end of the assignment. All in all, Spaulding had a ton to offer in terms of pathways to recovery, and I'm glad I took these chances in the long run.

After being bathed by towel and bucket for quite some time, I was told I was approaching a hygiene upgrade. I was moving up in the world, folks. My body, which now moved pretty okay on my left side, was ready for a shower chair. I still couldn't stand or move my torso, but the mobility in my arms and legs was improving rapidly. Thus, I was introduced to a giant, dark gray chair cushioned with plastic to repel water. It was a daunting sight, and my heart flipped like I was looking at a math test with questions that were undeniably more challenging than those we had studied. As with those tests, I had no choice but to face what was before me head-on.

With a hammock-like contraption, I was lifted and deposited into the chair. The nurses wheeled me into the giant bathroom, clearly built to handle these chairs, and removed my clothing. I was nervous.

As I've mentioned, the exposing of my pale and injured summer of 2014 body was no longer the cause of my fear; it was the uncertainty of what a shower would feel like.

Obviously I knew what showers felt like before my injury, when I could stand, but I didn't have that luxury anymore. This was entirely unpredictable, and I had no Nurse Suzi to crack a joke and ease my stress.

No, I had Nurse Mary. She is easily one of the sweetest women to ever exist. I have never met someone so passionate about what they do every day. Mary has the ability to wake up every morning knowing that she is having an effect on the lives of children and their families going through difficult times, and I believe that we are simply blessed to have her in this world with us. She possesses every trait I've ever hoped to have myself one day. The day I met her just happened to be action packed.

She warned that the shower water might be too hot or too cold and that with my hypersensitivity, I was the only one who could tell whether it was bearable for me. She was very comforting and informed me that she would back me out of it at any time. Feeling slightly more okay with the idea, I told her to start the water.

This was the weirdest feeling. The water struck my left side and felt like rain, but my right side felt nothing at all. As the water traveled from my head to my knees, I could feel the dividing line that split my body: half had impressive sensation and half had no trace of it. The water was mild on my left, but the sections of my skin where I was regaining sensation on my right felt like they were burning. I told her to shut off the water as soon as she had put shampoo in my hair. My hair is oily anyways, so it probably didn't do too much damage.

We wheeled out of the bathroom and got me redressed. I felt partly ashamed, but more relieved that the trial was over. I knew we'd be trying it again the next day, but the few-seconds-long encounter I had had with water that day was far long enough. Nurse Mary tucked me into bed afterward and stayed in my room for a little while.

She asked me questions about my injury and we talked about the strangeness of it all. I'm not sure if it was the shower experience specifically or the trust I had in anyone whose job was to redress me in the tight clothes I had to wear to help my circulation, but I ended up confiding in her. I told her about my parents, my brother, my friends, likes and dislikes. I told her about my debilitating fear of living the rest of my life with paralysis. I told her that I didn't know how others could do it.

She spent the entire afternoon in my room. She has this incredible laugh, and she laughed at most of my jokes. I wanted to hear the laugh more, so I told more jokes. By the time we were both laughing, the conversation had risen from its depressing start. We talked about everything from our darkest fears and her children to middle school, my friends, and their crushes.

Mary was amazing. My mom once asked me if she was the Spaulding equivalent of Suzi, but she wasn't. The two women were very different and were both necessary for the specific time of my recovery that they were a part of. I ended up doing my seventh-grade "change-maker" project about Mary because I was so desperate to show my gratitude.

My dad has played guitar and sung to me for as long as I can remember. He's never played in a band or anything, but I'm sure in an alternate universe he was a successful musician—his voice is really that good. Maybe I'm extremely biased because this is the same voice that put me to sleep and calmed me down in my early childhood, but I will never not stop whatever I'm doing to listen to him play and sing. At some point during my stay at Spaulding, he brought his guitar down.

I think some of my nurses fancied him a bit as was, but the guitar must've given off some sort of siren call. Nurses gathered in my room when they heard it. He and I spent hours some afternoons singing our favorite Bruno Mars and Carrie Underwood songs. The guitar was just another vessel that allowed us to forget about things for the duration of a song, and anything that yielded that power was magical.

I had played the trumpet in band back in the fifth and sixth grade, and I asked my parents to bring it along on their next trip from home to the hospital. They did, and I was overwhelmingly curious about whether I could play with my left hand.

If you aren't familiar with the construction of a trumpet, you won't necessarily know that the instrument is not built for the finger buttons to be pressed by a left hand. There are slots for fingers specifically on the right side, so I was skeptical about the whole endeavor. To my surprise, I was able not only to hit the buttons without too much difficulty, but to play all the notes I had originally learned with my right hand. This baffles my family to this day, but there must be a section of the brain that can transfer that knowledge from the right hand to the left. Weirdly enough, it almost felt natural.

I kept playing for a while when I returned to school, using both my left hand and bad posture to make the correct sounds. I gave up eventually because carrying the case around was a drag and I was running out of time to practice after school because of therapy, but I do sometimes pull it out and play an old tune.

By the end of middle school I actually ended up picking up my father's guitar a bit and playing it myself. He taught me basic chords, and I figured that I didn't need to use my right fingers to strum, just my wrist. I learned quickly and now often play the guitar at my school's benefit concerts. I now own two guitars and play them with very little difficulty, despite my paralysis.

I've always loved music. I grew up in living rooms with ballroom-style dancing to Michael Bublé and other crooner singers. My tastes have evolved over time, as most people's do, but that style of music sang me to sleep through my iPod some nights in the hospital, so it's very near to my heart.

I was never very exclusive when it came to the genre of music that I listened to. One of my friends had actually invited me over to her house to be an extra in a music video being filmed in her garage and around town with the band moe. I agreed without hesitation, and the video was published on the GotMoeVEVO YouTube channel while I was at Spaulding. The song is titled "Blonde Hair and Blue Eyes," and if you're really so inclined to watch it, I appear at 3:51 in a scarily close-up shot where I turn my head in fear. When we got the message that the video had been published, we pulled it up online almost immediately. This was the first time I had looked back on any sort of image or video of myself from before the injury, so it was disheartening to see myself in the footage, unaware of how my life would soon be flipped upside down. Nevertheless, the video is really kinda cool, and I don't regret joining in on that day in the slightest.

My mom and I watched a lot of TV to pass the time at Spaulding. We had just started the ABC drama *Revenge* on Netflix before my injury, so we decided that we might as well finish the series with all of the binge time we had available. We'd sit together in the crammed hospital bed for nights on end, watching the show. The show was distracting, and late at night I needed distractions. Late at night was always when my mind would race with every thought I could have about what was going on because I was used to analyzing my life in the shower and I didn't have that time to think anymore. Watching *Revenge* or plugging earbuds into my iPod for crooner classics was my way of shifting my focus. I'd have a lifetime to overanalyze what happened to me, and I didn't need to do that yet.

I still think about everything all the time. The injury affects just about everything I do and every decision I make in some way. I need to go down staircases with my right foot first and blow-dry and brush my hair with the same hand. I've figured so much out by now, but the whys and the hows still fascinate and bewilder me.

Just the other day while folding laundry I came across a pair of tall white socks. I had an immediate flashback to the knee-high compression socks I wore throughout my time at Tufts and then at Spaulding to assist my blood circulation. Catherine always told me that they looked just like Ariana Grande's knee-highs and that they were thusly fashionable, but I was less of a fan. They were purposely very tight, which made taking them on and off an obvious struggle for my parents and the nurses. They were also this light beige color that made my legs look like a doll's. My complaints about the socks around Mary gave me the "fashionista" nickname that the nurses would use for me, but I never took offense, considering my wardrobe still consisted of oversized T-shirts and loose shorts. Toward the times that my mom and I would go to the mall, the nurses were giving me input on what I should purchase.

When I was first starting to walk, a gentleman came to the therapy room with a concrete-like substance to make a mold for a hard plastic leg brace that would prevent my knee from snapping backward every time I took a step. He could make it in any color you could want, similar to a cast, but I went with my skin tone. I know, if I could go back in time, I would tell myself to get the tie-dye one too. The guy who made the brace ended up delivering it with a little *Iron Man* sticker because of my last name, so it wasn't too lame. Anyways, when it came to my newfound exploration into clothes that I liked, shoes were a must.

I had been wearing the same pair of sneakers that I had run track in for therapy until this point. However, the brace would add an extra inch to the length of my right foot. So, I had to buy every pair of shoes in two sizes: a women's 9 and a women's 12. I ended up wearing the plastic brace for most of my seventh-grade year, so this inconvenience was around for a while. The brace was uncomfortable, but it would have been significantly worse had I tried to fit it in any smaller size. I alternated between two uneven pairs of Converse for the rest of the year, so it was never a major issue. Suzi actually liked them.

Nurse Suzi visited me at Spaulding unexpectedly one day after a bike ride, and I was so grateful to see her. I knew that she had affected my life greatly, but I had no idea that I had enough of a similar effect on her to have her stop by. She told me that all the nurses still make fun of her for her *Family Feud* answers, which I couldn't help but be proud of. She was astonished by how far I'd come, and all I can think while writing this is that I can't wait for her to see me now.

From the day that I stood up for ten minutes with Krista onward, I had to drink a lot of fluids. The doctors suggested that I drink sixty-four ounces of Powerade or Gatorade on a daily basis. They also mentioned that people should drink that amount of water on a daily basis anyways, but I had always been bad at keeping up with liquids in sports and through the school day. When my friends cleaned out my sixth-grade locker, they found a museum of barely sipped water bottles. The necessity of it just had never occurred to me, so this was definitely karma from the fluid gods.

Turns out, when the hospital has only the blue flavor of Powerade available and you have to drink about three bottles' worth a day, it becomes sickening really fast. I had blue Powerade at every therapy session, with every meal, and with whatever came between. My dad thought it was funny to put the bottles at the end of the hallways so that every time I walked a little more, I could reward myself with Powerade. It really was one of the most disgusting things, probably second only to the Chinatown McD's. I hadn't minded the flavor beforehand; it was entirely because of the ludicrous amount of it that I had to consume. There is not a whole lot I wouldn't do before having to drink that pungent, syrupy taste again.

My dad got a kick out of adding humor to my therapy sessions. Krista always went along with it too, so they formed a bit of a comedy duo before all was said and done. In the occupational therapy room were little plastic farm animals that young children would practice walking to in the halls. Of course, I was about five years too old to fall for that incentive. Nonetheless, my dad would put the cows and sheep on the railings and make animal sounds every time I'd pass one. This made Krista burst into tears with laughter. Okay, I was laughing too.

I must let you know something about my dad. Even though we laughed a lot and use humor to our advantage through everything, we also went through the sadness as sincerely as anyone could. One night, my back was aching tremendously. I thought that I could relieve the pressure by flipping over onto my side. Apparently if you're in a bed for days on end, your back starts getting unbearably sore. It must have been 3:00 a.m. by the time I finally succeeded in hurling my back over my right arm. Instead of landing on my side, I fell flat on my stomach. I tried to undo this action, but I couldn't push myself enough to turn over. I'm not sure if this is because of claustrophobia or a fear of uncertainty, but I felt trapped by my own chest.

I yelled for my dad in the most panicked state I'd been in so far. He pounced off the couch to flip me back over, but I was genuinely overcome with the irrational fear of never being able to turn over again. I don't know why such a small, harmless thing triggered such an all-encompassing terror within me. It was probably a culmination of more than just that moment, but I was really afraid of getting myself into an irreversible position. Good thing that fear doesn't apply on a larger scale.

Many members of my community followed my story through my mother's Facebook posts on a Haley's Healing account she had made to inform everyone about what was going on during one of the very first days. Here's the unspoken truth about the page. I hated it.

All I wanted was privacy. My mom, with good intentions, I know, had taken selfies from my iPod Touch to add to her page. She wrote about what doctors were telling my parents before I even knew what was going on. I was deeply resentful toward my mother for a long time after the creation and continuation of the posts.

I often asked her to take the page down, but she would combat my arguments with the love, prayer, and attention she and I were receiving as a result of it. In a fit of helplessness and rage one night, I logged in to the account on our iPad and erased many of the images and posts. I was more accepting of its existence toward the end of my stay at Spaulding. I compromised with my mom one night by asking her if I could write the posts myself. Of course, I only ever wrote one because I still hated the lack of privacy associated with sharing my story with the world before the story was close to being over. The following was my post:

It's been five weeks and I finally wanted to compose tonight's update myself. I first would like to thank everyone for everything they have done to support my family and me. I truly believe the quick speed of my recovery wouldn't be possible without the love and prayer I constantly receive from this community. I am making strides every day with the help of the staff here at Spaulding, you all at home, and that competitiveness I knew would come in handy one day.

Two days ago I was on a canoe in the harbor, yesterday I played my trumpet with my left hand, today I threw a softball with my dad. Not only am I beginning to do things independently, but I'm also beginning to do the things I love. I have been able to visit with some of my close friends recently and it's nice to simply show them where I am and that I am still myself.

The minimal physical disabilities aside, I am beyond fortunate to be able to laugh and communicate, to have my personality, to still be Haley Stark. I now realize for many innocent children that is not always the case. I run sprints, but as my dad said at Tufts, this is a marathon. This is also a marathon that I will complete and I am currently in the final laps. I am so grateful that my future remains so positive and that I have such an outstanding group of people surrounding me.

I am hoping to write the majority of updates from now on as I progress, though in this post in particular I wanted to thank you all personally. I knew Falmouth was a special town, though judging by the way everyone united throughout the past month or so and made such a difference to my family and me, it is clear my followers and the people of Falmouth are far more special than I could have ever imagined. I cannot wait until I can thank you in person when I come home. I am doing better each day as the 'coming home date' approaches and will keep you posted. (6/3/2014)

Huh, I guess that about summarizes this book. Thank you, twelve-year-old Haley, you just gave me a great college essay option. I appreciate it.

I think the true reason I despised the posts so much may have been less about the privacy and more about the inaccuracies in them. The content all checked out in terms of medical situations, but the way that my mom tried to capture how I was feeling was simply done incorrectly.

I respect and appreciate her desire to have an outlet to the town, but that wasn't what *I* needed. What we found out three years later is that I needed to write a book to satisfy my desire to speak out to everyone, not a Facebook page. That's ultimately what compelled me to publish a memoir: I wanted my story, written out, completely from my own perspective. This is important to note as well because by the same token, I have absolutely no idea what it would be like to be the parental figure in that situation. I cannot begin to imagine myself in any other role than the one I had to take on. I don't know what it was like to be a close friend of mine, anxiously awaiting every update that went out. It'd be wrong of me to assume otherwise. I only know what you'll read throughout this book. I am grateful to my mom for documenting the chronology as well as she did.

Another interesting development through social media was the #HaleysHealing. I was more fond of the hashtag because it was the means by which many of my friends and their families shared their support with me. There was a time where a thousand posts on Instagram had the hashtag and I felt super popular. The alliterative, catchy phrase "Haley's Healing" has no definitive origin. Whoever came up with it should have gotten it trademarked, though, because it was virtually everywhere.

As the end of my stay at Spaulding was nearing, my mom and I sometimes convinced the nurses to let us go on "therapeutic days off," which just meant an opportunity to book it for the day and go to the giant Galleria Mall near the hospital. Shopping therapy is still totally therapy, especially for a mom and her twelve-year-old daughter.

We'd pack up the wheelchair in her trunk and sit me in the front of her car. The sensation of being in a car was terrifying. For whatever reason, after not being in a car for a while, the near nonexistent feeling of the car's speed becomes way more noticeable. I felt like I was on a roller coaster, being jolted in all directions with every turn. This is maybe because my body had become very accustomed to lying in a bed or slouching in a chair. Maybe my mom is just an awful driver, who knows (just kidding, Mom).

The Galleria Mall was great for shopping because there's every chain retailer a young girl could need within a pretty glass elevator's distance of each other, and all of my favorite stores were included. The mall was also swarmed with people, so nobody took a second glance at me in a wheelchair. I was as noticeable as the girls I'd pass with piercings and bright yellow hair or the boys on skateboards. The environment was sweaty, crowded, and super uncomfortable, but boy, was it welcoming.

The only exception was one interaction we had with a woman on the elevator once. The woman had bleached blond hair and had an intimidating way about her. Just as my mom rolled me into the confined box, the woman asked what had happened to me. I seriously considered ignoring her and letting her come to her own conclusions, but there would be a good three or four floors of awkwardness if that was the choice I made. I think I was considering the Kourtney Kardashian interview move where instead of answering the highly personal question she was asked, she just pretended to be frozen.

I decided to answer her, trying to assume that this stranger was genuinely curious with good intentions, but I didn't give her the facts, let's just say. I responded with a sigh and said, "Sports." She then asked which sport, even though I had been done with this conversation an answer ago. I said, "Beach volleyball, actually," to which my mom let out a snort of laughter. The woman apologetically explained that she knew exactly what I was going through because she had sprained her ankle once falling off a bike. This only prompted me to engage further. I now had an identity I had to uphold. I told her that my spandex had gotten caught in the net, since that was the most ridiculous cause of an injury involving beach volleyball that I could conjure up on the spot. My mom was laughing hysterically at this point, and the woman had to get off before she could come up with a response to this. That minute-long conversation took the day from good to great, and we hadn't even gotten to the Cheesecake Factory yet.

I also got to snag a therapeutic day off for the Fourth of July. We were planning on going to the Portland Sea Dogs baseball game that I had gone to each year to watch fireworks since before I can remember, but the game was rained out. A bunch of my friends were going to meet me there, but we had to quickly rearrange plans. So, we all met at FHOP, the pizza joint that sponsored all of our Little League teams growing up. I got to see more people I hadn't seen yet, as well as some of the people who had visited me a few weeks earlier. I showed off my standing to them all, and everyone was thrilled with my progress. The squad was back together again for a brief yet meaningful glimpse of what awaited me at home.

During the actual Fourth of July, I had planned on watching more *Revenge* with my mom instead of doing anything remotely patriotic. Not because I don't love my country or anything, I was just pretty beat from the night before and hadn't had any Fourth-related plans. That was until one of my nurses knocked on my door and invited me to come down to the parents' lounge. The parents' lounge had an unwritten rule about not allowing kids in, but it had the best view of Fenway Park, and apparently the fireworks had commenced. I decided after a few minutes of regretful hesitation to wheel down the hallway. What I saw in that room was the most moving display I have ever witnessed.

Almost every kid had congregated in the small room, each with their face pressed against the glass walls to see the lights. Parents stood a few feet behind them all, watching their children glowing, not the fireworks. Even a kid who spoke a language I was never able to identify was there, and I had never seen him move out of his room. He had a halo-type brace holding his neck and head in place, yet there was still an arch in his back when he leaned toward the show in the sky.

Shayna and Samuel giggled along as they tried to explain to each other which crackling sounds were their favorites. They realized that their voices were unable to replicate the sounds of any one firework in particular, and gave up by agreeing that they were all magnificent.

I can't say that I was watching the lights or the children. I think I was watching the space as a whole. I was absorbing the relief of parents who all looked equally dazed and in distress. I was taking in the positivity of the children, and the incredible strength it must've taken for them all to find happiness in light of whatever they were going through that had put them there. It was an indescribably beautiful army of young souls who stood and sat side by side in front of that glass, with goodness radiating from their bodies. No evil in the universe could ever take down their fortress of power and will. They were the chosen ones, the ones who would live their lives disadvantaged in some way because of a childhood illness or injury, but they were also the ones who would live their lives knowing that they are unstoppable beings who fought like hell in the face of pain and frustration.

The children at Spaulding are there through no fault of their own. The families there suffer beneath the everlasting cloud of uncertainty that dwells over that facility, but they are strong and they will prevail. I wish more than I can describe that I could explain this feeling to you, but I recognize and respect that I cannot. I try to believe that I had this injury because something above me knew I could handle it. I hope that something above me knew I'd do good because of it. I spent days on end staring at photos of my friends on bulletin boards, hoping that I was taking this one for the team—that they would never have to go through anything like this and knowing that for any of them, I'd do it all again in a heartbeat.

I've learned how to love people in a way that I could have never conceived of. I write this in my room with tears dripping on my computer keyboard, hoping that you understand my admiration for the people who are directly involved with the healing of sick children. I thank a God I'm not even sure I believe in fully that I was given my health again. I watched as brain-damaged three-year-olds sat in chairs with empty eyes and lost families. I am infinitely grateful that I have who I am still, because that is stripped from the children who lay around me on the floors of both Spaulding and Tufts. I got to go home, and so many children will not have that same fate. I was ready to go home, but I will never be ready to leave those places behind.

Braydon ended up traveling all the way up from Rhode Island with flowers he had picked from his garden to surprise me when I was discharged about two weeks after the Fourth. Brooke was wheeled out with two big pigtails and the biggest smile I'd ever seen. Shayna and Samuel emerged from their rooms, and I was able to get out of my chair and walk out of the double doors I had lived behind for so many days. That was always my goal: to walk out of Spaulding. I had seen a kid walking out when I first arrived and envied his mobility. The very concept of walking out drove me to make it happen. I hoped that some other kid saw me leaving so that they could do the same.

Life Afterward

Seventh grade was ready to begin. At this point, I had a brace all the way up my leg, I was arguably not ready to be off a walker, but I was anyways, and I had a cast-type brace on my arm. Despite these accessories, I was determined to fit in. I know—how lame.

I am now going into my junior year of high school, and I still think that seventh grade is one of the most difficult years in a young adult's life. There is an incredible pressure to somehow both fit in with those around you and learn who you are as an individual and what makes you different. These are wildly contradictory goals, which make focusing on much of anything else pretty difficult.

I remember walking through the seventh-grade hallway for the first time. Perhaps I was just extremely aware of my surroundings and quick to notice people, but it certainly felt as though I was being stared at. I expected some degree of this, considering that I hadn't seen the majority of my classmates since May and most people had some idea about the severity of my injury. Still, it was a bit scary. I imagine this is what people who use a wheelchair every day must feel like when they're stared at by totally kind-spirited people just because they have some physical indication of an injury. I'm lucky enough now to live without anything that makes me appear as though I've had an injury like a stroke, aside from a little limp. My right hand doesn't have a brace anymore, so I often meet people today with little to no understanding of my physical conditions.

I remember that classes weren't very challenging and that I was able to get right back into the courses even though I had missed a few months in sixth grade. I wanted to join sports again and continue recovering at the same rate at which I'd recovered over the summer. I wanted the life that I had had before my injury, but that wasn't what was ahead of me. I joined the track team, but in a new role.

Mr. D suggested that I help out with coaching. I decided I'd try it out, and I ended up doing paperwork for the team, completing spreadsheets, and traveling with the team to the basketball court in Portland where the meets were held. I wasn't running, obviously, but I was there. What I was actually doing probably sounds unexciting, but I loved every second of it. I was participating, and I was necessary to a team. I still wore the shirt every school day that we'd have a meet, and I still felt included. It certainly pained me to watch others live out what had once been my reality, but it was all worth it to be there. I continued this through my eighth-grade year as well and stayed dedicated to the team. They were still my people after all that time, and track was still my passion after all that change.

Aside from track, I had ended my involvement in all other sports. I still quickly realized that my injury would not keep me from a lot of the things that most thirteen-year-olds go through in middle school. I still liked boys, went to school dances, had friend drama, and lived life like a typical young teenager in many ways. The only major difference at this time, it felt, was that I went to New England Rehab in Portland once a week or so to try to walk without a brace or use my right hand.

The braces brought about a bit of insecurity, but I was always very realistic with myself when I'd remind myself how necessary they all were. Of course, I wanted to be free of the braces and wanted to worry about other parts of my body aside from my nerve damage, but I was okay with it for the most part. This was a part of my life that will permanently affect me on a daily basis, and I should never hide that.

During the fall season, I called my two friends Catherine and Claudia for help. I had been experiencing an uncomfortable and uncontrollable anxiety, knowing that the pediatric floor at Spaulding would still be crowded around the holidays, if not more so. I had no idea how I could possibly help, but I was ready to figure something out.

I conducted some research about what it takes to start a nonprofit and the variety of ways in which people have gone about starting organizations. I knew that with school and my own recovery still going on, I wanted something rather small scale. The results were anything but.

I decided I wanted to raise money to purchase gifts for the children at Spaulding. I contacted the child-life specialist who worked there, and she was thrilled by the idea. We organized fund-raisers at the school, including a before-school drive where my friends and I stood with plastic cartons outside the school near the student drop-off in freezing weather. We wore Santa hats and sang carols, and it seemed more students remembered to bring a dollar than they ever had for any of the other fund-raisers we had held through the student council. With the combination of that drive, a school dance and other events organized by the council, Catherine, Claudia, and myself, we raised over a thousand dollars. That may not seem like much, but it was a brilliant start to our project.

We then decided to expand our goal by talking with my mom, who owns a restaurant in Falmouth. We held a fund-raiser night there with a raffle and a percentage of the proceeds going to our group. We spread the word about the night with as much passion as we could, and it ended up being shockingly busy. Some people just stopped in to give us donations.

When it came to formulating what we would put in the gift boxes, we decided to divide the groups into younger and older girls, and younger and older boys. Everything we purchased fit our requirements. All of the gifts were new, many were soft, all were fragrance-free, and all could be enjoyed without having to move.

We filled almost thirty large gift bags with toys, lotions, books, and various other presents. Some bags included Pillow Pets and Alex and Ani bracelets, so these were some high-demand finds. One day, we went to

Walmart and filled two carts with blankets and other last-minute gifts. There, one person approached us and assumed we were donating it all. They ended up giving us a donation on the spot. We ended up spending the entirety of what we had raised, but nothing more. It really couldn't have gone better.

We called ourselves Spaulding Santas and traveled to Charlestown to hand deliver all the gift bags. There are only ever twelve or thirteen kids on the floor, so there were some leftovers for the children who would come in the following weeks. The day was overflowing with emotions. I was walking in that hallway again but not for myself so much as for people who were trying to do the same. My friends were absolute angels, and I couldn't have done it without them. We did the same thing the next year, and stopped freshman year to break off into our own, more specific service interests. I started putting this book together around the fall of that year and knew right off that a percentage of the proceeds would go toward the National Spinal Cord Injury Association. This book was my next step toward finding my place in the world of giving back.

I've never really thought far into why I was experiencing that anxiety about the children being at Spaulding during the holidays. Perhaps the memory of the handicap-accessible playground was so prominent in my subconscious that when snow fell, my first thought was about a cover of thick white restricting the kids from using the equipment. Maybe the Bublé I had listened to nightly for over forty nights at Spaulding reminded me of my living room, his Christmas album, and freedom. Maybe I wanted kids to dance to Bublé in their living rooms instead of suffering in hospital chairs within the confines of Spaulding, or even Tufts or Maine Med for that matter. Maybe I'm too idealistic.

To be honest, I've avoided thinking much about it, because it frightens me. In the same way that I am bitterly afraid of having to go through another stroke or something similar, it terrifies me to know that there are children at Spaulding 24/7. I try to give a moment to think about it every day, but it's crushing. There's no valid excuse not to, but perhaps one of my biggest secrets is that my heart hurts on a nightly basis when the idea of those children slips into my mind.

Thinking about them at Spaulding is still better than thinking about them at Tufts. The kids in the PICU at Tufts are also always there and always in critical condition. My mind will wander from facility to facility until I think about the kids with parents who would've listened to the doctors at Maine Medical and put them on life support, never to come off. Worse yet, I think of the first ambulance and the EMTs who picked me up. What happens to the kids who would've supposed a pull in their shoulder was just that: a pull, something that could be napped off with Advil? What happens to the kids who don't have insurance and can't afford treatment?

I am one of the lucky ones. I could have had it so much worse. The universe paved a path to recovery for me that was complicated, unique, and very fortunate. When I stress about my right hand or have flashbacks to four years ago, something that digs me out of the holes I can fall into is the perspective I have since seeing children younger, weaker, and way worse off than I have been. Sure, I break down sometimes. I curse the skies above every time I walk near the track field at our high school and imagine my quick, healthy legs racing. I still wish that my right hand will magically start moving every time I find a four-leafed clover or lose an eyelash. There are easy days and there are harder days, and I have to take on each wholeheartedly in order to get by and stay above it. I try to keep strong so that every day at school and in general life, I can work toward pursuing a career that will help these children somehow. I've been given that chance when so many haven't, and I can only believe that there's a reason I was given it.

At New England Rehab I still experienced depressing thoughts and discouragement every now and again, but they were always quickly overpowered by the optimism that still shone through my family.

During physical therapy here, I practiced walking down hallways without my walker and with various other types of crutches. I practiced getting up off of the ground so that I could do it if I were to fall. It took quite a few sessions before I was even remotely successful. We attached electrodes to my right leg to try to stimulate mobility while I'd walk, but they were more painful than anything else. They did work on my hand well.

We spent a long time working with my hand and electrodes in occupational therapy. Every time they would shock my hand, my nerves would spike up and the fingers would start to move. I gradually figured out how to work the machine myself and brought it into the school year to use during class periods when I wasn't moving much. I think the fact that I was being electrocuted every few seconds creeped out some of my peers, which was amusing.

Even though my recovery had plateaued a bit, I went from being in two large leg braces in a walker to having just a one-handed crutch with the braces to having just the braces. After the seventh-grade school year, I hardly even needed the braces anymore.

The one-handed crutch was wonderful. It was small, easy to use, and made me seem way less like a grandmother than the walker did (not that I don't love grandmothers, I just didn't want to be one when I was thirteen). Delaney and I ended up naming the crutch Axela, which was a strange variation of my crush's name for some bizarre reason, so it was assisting my comfort in not only a physical sense but also in a joking, mental sense.

By the time theatre rolled around, I was ready to join and restart my passion for acting as well. Theatre is something that you can always do, whatever condition you may be in. I felt safe, expressive, and useful there. I felt like I belonged among the others involved.

Theatre inspired me to take leaps that I wouldn't have otherwise. I ran for student council vice president and won, then president my eighth-grade year. I knew just about every staff member at the school and felt as though I had conquered the world.

At some point in the eighth grade, I stopped therapy for the most part. I tried acupuncture, but it didn't seem to help all that much. Besides, I had seen the *SNL* acupuncture skit, and even after a few sessions I still thought my blood could go spewing out of those needles at any second. That decision was a blurry combination of realizing that my recovery was pretty much in my hands because I could walk and move my arms well, and wanting to live life as independently as possible. I spent some time at OrthoAssociates in Portland, a sports-oriented rehab facility, with both physical and occupational therapy, but neither lasted very long. I felt some pressure to keep up with therapies, but I was thrilled with the progress I had made and wanted to adjust to school and life as a braceless, mobile student.

My walking improved just by moving about the school and my homes to such an extent that my limp is pretty hard to spot now. Eighth grade would let me explore who I was as a new human being, with only the setbacks of minor paralysis in my leg and hip and a paralyzed right hand. The administration at the middle school made every accommodation I could possibly need, and Catherine's locker was moved next to mine so that she could help me carry my books around. She acted like this was a pain sometimes, but I think she secretly enjoyed the unlimited excuse for being late to class that I was giving her.

Everyone was always willing to help out. At some point in the year, I persuaded my locker buddy to date me. David was incredible. With my lack of mobility, I often felt like a burden to him. I was always very afraid that he was annoyed by having to carry my textbooks or tie my shoes when they'd come undone, but he reassured me constantly that it was never a big deal and that he'd help out whenever and wherever I needed him to. I know, right? What a catch.

We ended up going to our school's "boat dance" together—Falmouth's equivalent of an eighth-grade graduation. We danced through the night to early 2000s songs that the DJ insisted on playing, and I can pretty honestly say that I forgot about my injury for the evening.

David to this day is one of my biggest fans. He never hesitates to pick up a phone call or carry two backpacks if I appear to be struggling with my own. I was really blessed with the people I had in my life after the injury. I can say with no doubt that everyone, whether I knew them before or not, really loved me.

Freshman year of high school is a transitional period for any young adult. Thrown into an environment with new teachers, many of whom I wasn't sure had heard of the green ribbons or my injury, and three years of students above me, I was admittedly a bit anxious. However, I very quickly attached to the administrators and made relationships that will last me my lifetime.

There was one particular day that changed everything for me and brought about an entirely new and refreshing peace to my existence. Oddly enough, the day was defined by what most would probably consider a humiliating display.

Our theatre company at Falmouth High School participates in a regional festival annually with a one-act that showcases the best of our acting, directing, lighting, sound, and set/wardrobe design in about thirty-five minutes. Each year, auditions are held where you can perform a monologue of your choosing, usually one that matches the tone of the show, although that isn't required, and see if you're called back to read portions of the script. As a freshman, I was very much under the influence of the unwritten rule that underclassmen rarely appear on the festival stage. However, I eventually brought myself to figure that this rule meant only that I could audition without the accompanying anxiety of wanting to get a role.

So I auditioned. I had no idea what the show we were going to do was, and I auditioned using a comedic monologue I had found online about a woman who was asked to watch her friend's obnoxious puppy. I read it in a New York accent and incorporated physicality, which would have mortified middle school Haley. Of course, I quickly discovered that we were doing a serious and famous piece cut down from *The Little Foxes* by Lillian Hellman, but that was after the fact.

Oddly enough, when the callback list was posted a few weeks later, my name was on it. I didn't end up getting a part in the show, which I was perfectly content with, but I was on "running crew," which meant that I'd have to attend every rehearsal to be a maid in the background. It doesn't sound glamorous now that I'm seeing it written out, but this experience was pivotal in my self-discovery so far. I was forced into befriending students in the grades above me who all worked on the show, and I couldn't be more grateful that I did.

In this crowd of older kids who I thought I'd run and hide from were my current best friends. I wouldn't say that my story has come full circle, because I'm now left at a place much greater than where I began. I am empowered, enriched, and thankful. While working on the festival, I moved furniture, stayed up late, and continued my schoolwork just like everyone around me. I formed a bond with my friends Kade, Lauren, Oscar, Sarah, Nellie, and Sophie B. that will never be broken. They give me the light and glory I've found at the end of the tunnel. Not unlike the song we used to sing in Girl Scouts, I've been completely immersed in the notion of making new friends but keeping the old. Claudia, Catherine, Lila, Jessica, Ike, Sophie G., and Delaney still give me the love and warmth that they gave me while I was overcoming this injury. In a totally purposeful, pretentious fashion, I can tell you that I have it all.

Although I began writing this by mentioning my disbelief in the existence of an "end," I still feel like finding closure for various pieces of your life story is important. My injury will always affect me, whether it's when a stranger goes to shake my hand or when I forget the blessing that lies within the skin that still limps down hallways. Nevertheless, there was a particular moment that defines my "closure" and gives me the best way to leave you all off of my story.

I met a kid named John in an improv club my freshman year. During the festival theatre season, I developed a major crush on him. Knowing someone only through improv and theatre gives you a weird perspective on their character, so to say I was shocked when I found out he liked me too would be a bit of an understatement. With immense help from the other cast and crew members, we eventually went out on a date.

While talking to him, I very quickly realized that he was completely unaware of my injury; maybe he just thought I was really bad at carrying chairs onto the stage or something. There had been a lot of community involvement around my injury when it happened three years earlier. However, John was older than I was and probably didn't have a reason to think the green ribbons still up around town were for me so long afterward. Let me tell you something, this was really awesome.

I had gone months knowing somebody from activities I was involved in, and he had no idea. In my mind, this began an era of my life where people didn't first associate who I was with a stroke. I was so overcome with pride and excitement, I could hardly let myself explain it at all. What I then figured out, though, was that explaining it wasn't nearly as dreadful as I'd thought it would be. Explaining it from my perspective was empowering in a way not unlike the feeling of belting out "The Climb" by Miley Cyrus when you're alone—I highly recommend doing that at least once if you haven't, by the way.

Giving my side of the story was life changing. Now I've shared it with you as well. I have written and rewritten the ending to this book of mine many times. I've tried clichés, quotes, poetry, and even photographs. I eventually came to the conclusion that none of these would give me the satisfaction I'd been searching for. So, I'll end this with a casual and genuine list of truths that define my world post-stroke.

I will never be able to understand what someone else is going through, and even by writing this book I will never be able to put someone else in my shoes. The adage of "putting yourself in someone else's shoes" is flawed and restrains us from appreciating our infinite differences as human beings.

Some people will always have it worse than you, and some people will always have it better. I will not allow the suffering of others to keep me from feeling sorry for myself from time to time. Nevertheless, my awareness of the beds that always have a waiting list of sick children at Spaulding and Tufts has taught me that there will never be a day when children and families alike aren't experiencing similar challenges.

People just want to hear that life sucks sometimes. You will not always have the magic words that can heal someone's sadness. Sometimes, just acknowledging the sucky-ness that's causing it helps. My sophomore biology teacher helped inspire this one.

Not having use of my right hand does not make any part of life impossible, nor does the limp in my right leg. The day I learned how to put my hair into a ponytail is the day I learned that I'm going to be just fine.

I am an incredible hypocrite. I preach advice to people as though I follow it myself and admit this to you in an honest and self-aware manner.

I need to work on this and recognize that perhaps the best advice anyone can receive is the advice they'd give out to others.

Life is full of crazy twists and turns. If someone had told me four years ago that I'd be living in my friend Molly's house with her family because our parents married, I wouldn't have believed it. However, just like the injury, this was a twist that I'm taking on with all my heart because I genuinely believe that a lot of goodness can come from this new experience.

The people in your life drift in and out of it for a reason.

You're never going to be everyone's best friend, but if you can be your own best friend, then you'll never be lonely. Yeah, I recognize how lonely that sounds—you don't have to tell me—but this is my truth, so it's fine.

I'm not afraid to apply to college next year, and neither should any other high schooler. I plan to apply early to Georgetown University in D.C., and as much as I really want to get in and study political science there, it won't be the end of the world if I don't get that opportunity. You can find greatness in anything.

You'll never be able to write down everything. I was very hesitant to say I had finished writing this book because I was very nervous that I had missed something major. What I've learned is that there is no way I could possibly share my entire experience with you all. So instead, I'll leave it to my audience to ask me questions so that I can more fully complete sections of this story. Yep, I'm putting that on you guys.

Laugh in the face of pain. Use your ability to laugh as a shield, as weaponry, and as a general survival kit. Mark Twain famously wrote,

"Against the assault of laughter, nothing can stand." I don't know much about Twain and I don't honestly remember a whole lot from reading *Huck Finn*, but he seems like a pretty smart guy, so I plan to listen to him.

When people ask to shake my hand, it's awkward for only a second. I can handle it and so can they. I wore braces on my hand for a while so that I could lie about my injury to make the story less complicated when I met people, but that is completely unnecessary. I am proud of where I've been, and I'm prepared to tell the world about it.

Surround yourself with people who make you laugh. This is where I have to give a shout-out to Billy, who suggested I title this book *A Stroke of Bad Luck*. Expose yourself to light and laughter, because there is too much sadness all around and it's so easy to find yourself in the dark.

Do the things that scare the hell out of you. My sophomore algebra teacher/high school track coach doesn't know it yet, but I fully intend to join the outdoor team my senior year. I've shown everyone else that I can thrive in the face of this injury, and that's how I'm going to show myself the same.

Some things in life are sprints, and others are marathons. Treat each accordingly.

Special Mentions

Susie Nick

Jessie Grearson

Dr. Adams

The Morrissette Family

The Rouhana Family

The Rogers Family

The Kiely Family

The Fallon Family

The Wimert Family

The Davis Family

The Legere Family

The Warnock Family

The Hepburn Family

The Tait Family

The Bonnvie Family

The Teufel Family

The Lara Family

The DeWolfe Family

The Bayer Family

The Carlisle Family

The Staff of Falmouth Middle School

The Staff of Falmouth Elementary School

The Staff of Falmouth High School

Coach Dissell

Zanne Langlois

Emily Stuart

Amy Magnuson

Meg Barry

Tammy Heathco

Daniel Paul

Craig Shain

Sara Jones

MaryBeth Bachman

Robin Haley

moe.

The Staff of Maine Medical Center

The Staff of Tufts Medical Center

The Staff of Spaulding Rehabilitation

The FHS Class of 2014

The Community of Falmouth, Maine

The Community of Cumberland, Maine

The Community of Portland, Maine

... and so many others

Letters

Something that was extremely important to me from the day I decided that I'd be publishing this memoir was the idea that I would not read anyone their sections of the book before publication. This was because I wanted the story to be as much from my perspective as possible with little influence from others.

In the same fashion, I asked a few of my loved ones to write about an experience they remember and told them that I would publish it without reading it first. So, I will be reading the following pieces when the book is first in my hands.

On a warm May afternoon, I began making dinner for my daughter, who had just returned from track practice. In moments, the first signs of what would later be confirmed as an extremely rare spinal cord stroke began to change the path for an amazing twelve-year-old girl. What initially presented as simple dehydration quickly escalated into every parent's worst nightmare. With blinding speed it became apparent that Haley's situation was anything but "simple."

After a brief stay at Maine Medical Center, consisting of frightening rounds of MRIs and other evaluative measures, the evidence revealed that my daughter had suffered a stroke. The brutal diagnosis changed her life and the lives of everyone who knows and loves her.

Seeking medical clarity and cutting-edge skill, Haley was transferred to Tufts

Medical Center in Boston. Her condition worsened rapidly. The inability to determine the origin of her injury, difficulty breathing, and onset of pneumonia forced me to come to grips with the sobering prospect of potentially losing my daughter.

Haley survived a hellish week of tests and procedures. She fought for her life with an unspoken will and courage that I have never witnessed. It occurred to me how easy it would have been for her to surrender. It has since occurred to me that that was never an option. I wish to offer my eternal thanks to the doctors and nurses at Tufts. There is no appropriate or adequate way to express my gratitude. You saved Haley's life.

The next phase came in the form of a forty-day stay at Spaulding Rehabilitation Hospital in Charlestown, Massachusetts. It was there that the slow, arduous process of recovery would begin. Arriving with barely any feeling in her extremities, Haley's future was at best uncertain. Over the next six weeks, every moment of my daughter's life was under scrutiny. Powerless to assist herself, Haley relied on the nurses and staff at Spaulding for her every need. At any hour for any reason, these selfless and compassionate people helped my daughter move forward and maintain dignity.

To watch a child fight to regain her life is humbling. To be surrounded by other children fighting the same fight is transformative. The hours of seeing Haley struggle to take a step or balance herself tore at my heart. The gains were slow to come. And then one day, Haley got my attention and stood from her wheelchair and sat on her bed. I knew at that moment I had witnessed a small but powerful act. For the first time her injury loosened its grip.

Four years have passed since that awful day. Through tireless rehabilitation and with a fierce positive energy, Haley claimed most of what had been taken. She returned to our loving community and has excelled in new avenues and interests. With the support of her teachers and administrators, Haley has become an academic leader. Her love of the arts is reflected in her participation in theatre. Her strong opinions are reflected in speech and debate.

As time has passed, I have finally reached a point where I go to bed and don't worry that something dreadful may happen the next day. I always thought it was my job to teach my children about life. I hope I've done that. The surprise is what my daughter has taught me. Her courage against formidable odds and her unrelenting desire and love of life has shown me how meaningful and precious each day truly is.

I look forward to the woman Haley will become, knowing there is no obstacle she cannot overcome or adversity she cannot stare down.

I love you limitlessly and will never need to look elsewhere for motivation. I love being your dad.

Dear Haley,

It's been just over four years since you suffered a spinal stroke and I experienced one of the scariest days of my life as a parent. Recalling that day and the days that followed gets easier because now it's as if I'm telling a story that doesn't belong to me. Some moments have faded into the mist of my clouded mind, and for that I am grateful. Time marches on, and events that seemed insurmountable have been conquered and life changing in ways I could have never imagined.

On May 21, 2014, you suddenly became very ill. I was unaware of what was happening until I received a call from your father that you were in the ER. I was told that everything would be fine and I didn't need to rush in. I rushed in. Here's what I remember about the moment I arrived... You were completely paralyzed from the neck down, you were choking on your own saliva and needed a cough assist machine to help you clear your airways, you were so scared and so was I. The doctors struggled to diagnose your symptoms before finally agreeing that you had had a rare spinal stroke.

In the wee hours of the morning one of the head physicians brought me into her office to tell me to prepare for the worst. You couldn't breathe and needed to be put on life support as soon as possible, and your chances for survival were slim. I sat in disbelief at the news, trying hard to maintain my composure and strength. How does a healthy, athletic twelve-year-old have a life-threatening spinal stroke out of the blue? It really didn't matter to me; the answer to that question never mattered to me. All that mattered was doing whatever had to be done to fix you, to make you well again.

So, in my shocked state, I looked the doctor in the eye and said, "No, you're not putting her on life support. You are putting her in an ambulance or on a plane and you're getting her to Boston as soon as possible. I want her in a hospital where she will receive the best care from physicians who know how to treat this." And, within a few hours a bed was found at Tufts and we were on our way.

Things did not get easier once we got there. As a matter of fact, things got much worse. Once we arrived at Tufts, more tests were run, and another MRI and countless other examinations were done to determine the cause of your stroke. You caught pneumonia and went on life support within twenty-four hours. Over the next few days, you were poked and prodded and hooked up to more wires and tubes than I've ever seen. You contracted the flu virus and, scariest of all, sepsis. I clearly remember one nurse saying, "If you don't know what that is, don't look it up. You need to trust that we have it under control." I didn't look it up.

Trust is an interesting concept. According to the dictionary, trust is "a firm belief in the reliability, truth, ability, or strength of someone or something." I decided to trust. I trusted that I had made the right decision to bring you to Boston, and I trusted that the doctors and nurses at Tufts were going to save you. And they did. You did your part too. You fought every day to get well. You were losing so much weight on your already slender frame. You were hungry, scared, and confused, and yet you continued to find the strength to fight for your recovery. It was amazing to witness.

When you finally turned the corner, after thirteen days in ICU, and were well enough to be transferred to Spaulding Rehab, a new fight began. You left Tufts on a hospital gurney, unable to get out of bed, unable to feed yourself very well, bathe yourself, or do any of the daily functions we take for granted. Watching your determination at Spaulding, your strength during the three-daily hour-long PT and OT sessions over nearly three months was so inspirational to so many. I've always said that I will be forever grateful to the staff at Tufts for saving your life and forever grateful to the loving, caring men and women at Spaulding for giving you back your mobility.

My dearest Haley, you closed your book with the fifteen things you learned from this experience so I'll close this letter the same way...

1. Your life can change in an instant; be grateful for every day.
2. Don't always accept what people in authority tell you. If your instincts tell you to question something, question it.

You are your strongest advocate. Speak up!

3. DO NOT GIVE UP! The only constant in life is change. Things will get better.

4. We are stronger than we know.

5. Community is so important. We are impacting those around us more than we realize. What you give to others will come back to you tenfold.

6. Treat others with kindness. It will always be returned to us when we least expect it and need it most.

7. During our darkest hours, we are never alone. Sometimes the people you least expect show up.

8. God is real and carries us when we are no longer able to walk on our own.

9. There is no greater love than the love a parent has for a child.

10. The millennial generation is pretty terrific.

11. Healing is a process. Be patient with yourself.

12. There are angels among us. Thank you, Nurse Suzi!

13. If you want a better life, it's up to you to create it.

14. Mind over matter. If you have a mind-set to accomplish something, nothing else matters. What you believe, you will achieve.

15. Finally, I know in my heart that for all my mistakes, I can be proud of my two greatest accomplishments: my son, Sam, and my daughter, Haley. You are both strong, kind, generous, intelligent, caring human beings who are making a difference in this world. It's a joy and a privilege to be a part of your journey. I can't wait to walk alongside you the rest of the way.

Haley, you came to me when I least expected it. You surprise me constantly and fill my heart with more love than I've ever deserved. I am so grateful that I get to be both your mom and your best friend. It's an incredibly rare gift to have such a strong mother-daughter bond, especially through your teenage years. Thank you for being you! Congratulations on telling your story. I am so very proud of you!!!

MOM

Haley,

Thirteen short years ago, we met in preschool after you asked me to play Polly Pockets. I agreed, unaware that it was the start to an incredible friendship. After that, we did everything together, from playing hair salon to T-ball and gymnastics every week. There was never a dull moment with us, whether it was dancing along to our all-time favorite song, "Sweet Escape" by Gwen Stefani, or sipping water out of wineglasses as we watched *Bachelor in Paradise*. We practically grew up together. You soon became my other sister, the Mary-Kate to my Ashley, if you will, and someone who would change my life forever. I can honestly say that my life would have been completely different if I hadn't met you.

I remember first hearing about what happened and thinking, *Haley will be fine. It's Haley.* I was confident that you could take on anything. (She did, in fact, fall off a swing and have to be taken away in an ambulance, but that's another story.) I was certain that if anyone could take on a challenge like this, it would be you. I was in shock, wondering how something like this could happen to someone who I ran against in Mr. Halligan's forty-yard dash just hours before, and who I spent every day of my childhood with.

I remember going to visit you at Spaulding, nervous that you wouldn't be the same after the stroke. But there you were, with a smile on your face, talkative as ever. That's when I knew I hadn't lost you, and that I was right. You faced this challenge and took it like a champ while continuing to have a positive attitude throughout. That's the Haley I know and love, and will never stop loving. You continue to blow me away every day, as I watch you battle balancing theatre, debate, classes, a social life, and extracurriculars every day. I honestly don't know how you do it. You have this drive, this special ability to push yourself to become just the greatest human out there.

Thank you for everything you have taught me, to never give up, to believe in myself, and to push myself. Never stop doing you, and never stop inspiring people just like me. Congratulations on everything you have and will achieve (especially this book). You deserve the world, don't ever let anyone stand in your way. I love you!

Love, Lila Rouhana

Haley and I have been through it all. Having known her for as long as I can remember, we've been there for each other through the triumphs (she's had many), the good days, the bad days, the breakups, the makeups, you name it. But this was something I never expected to go through with her. Someone who I had gone through so many things with was going through something so horrible on her own and I couldn't do anything about it. That destroyed me.

Things went by so slowly without her at school. I've always floated through friend groups throughout my entire school experience, but she was the constant that I knew I always had. Without her, I felt lost. When I went to visit her at Spaulding for the first time, I remember how nervous I felt on the train. Even with her cat staying at my house, I still felt like I wasn't doing enough, even though it was completely out of my control. I hate it when things are out of my control. Nonetheless, I packed up my One Direction posters, Scotch tape, and nail polish and headed to Spaulding. I will never forget that day.

It's absolutely mind blowing to me that it's been over four years. So much can happen in four years. The amount of things that Haley has overcome and accomplished throughout this time will never cease to amaze me. Her perseverance and drive are qualities of hers that I have envied for years. She is just so amazing. There is no other way to put it, she is just good at everything she does. She is one of the best actresses I have ever seen at our age (I'm patiently waiting for us to share the stage as an iconic duo). She knows how to make a film like no other. She is always on call to accompany me on guitar (even if it's "Ivy" by Frank Ocean, for the sixth time). Her grades are unreal. But overall, she is a good friend. This hasn't always been true of me, but even then, she was nothing but good to me. I know that she is there for me no matter what happens, through it all.

xo, Jes

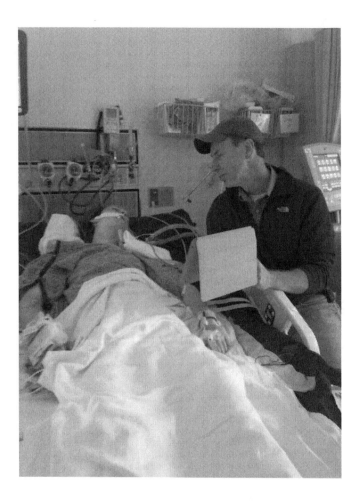

My dad and me watching old SNL reruns on my iPad
while at Tufts Medical Center.

JUNE

S	M	T	W	T	F	S
1	2	3	4	5	6	7
8	9	10	11	12 TP105	13	14
15	16	17	18	19	20	21
22 THIS MONTH	23	24	25	26	27	28
29	30					

JULY

S	M	T	W	T	F	S
		1	2	3	4	5
6	7	8	9	10	11	12
13	14	15	16	17	18	19
20	21	22	23 HOME	24	25	26

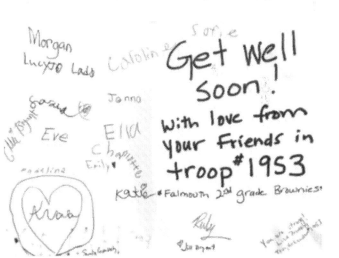

Morgan
Lucy70 Lads Caroline Sofie

Get Well soon!

Janna

Sarah

Eve Ella

Charlotte

Emily

Katie

With love from your Friends in troop #1953

Falmouth 2nd grade Brownies

Araa

WE LOVE YOU
you
Haley

Get

Well Soon

HALEY

!!

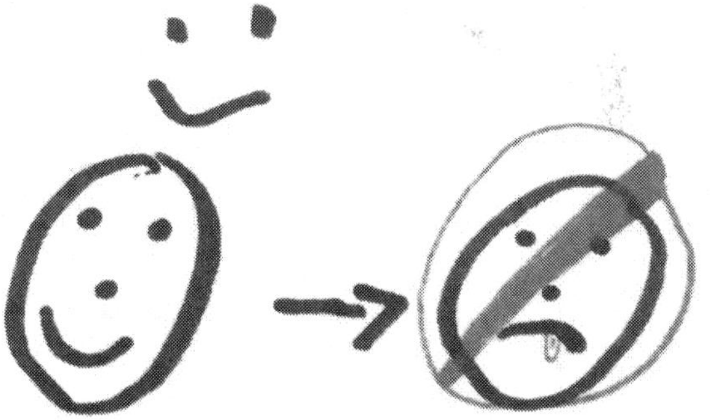

Get Better!!

your my
bestfriend

I ♥ U

SOR

I ♥ U

because Love, Lila

To: the wonderful Hailey Stark